Hands-On G Suite for Administrators

Build and manage any business on top of the Google Cloud
infrastructure

Cesar Anton Dorantes

BIRMINGHAM - MUMBAI

Hands-On G Suite for Administrators

Commissioning Editor: Pavan Ramchandani
Acquisition Editor: Prachi Bisht
Content Development Editor: Shubham Bhattacharya
Technical Editor: Rudolph Almeida
Copy Editor: Safis Editing
Project Coordinator: Nusaiba Ansari
Proofreader: Safis Editing
Indexer: Manju Arasan
Graphics: Jisha Chirayil
Production Coordinator: Nilesh Mohite

First published: March 2019

Production reference: 1290319

Published by Packt Publishing Ltd.
Livery Place
35 Livery Street
Birmingham
B3 2PB, UK.

ISBN 978-1-78961-301-8

www.packtpub.com

`mapt.io`

Mapt is an online digital library that gives you full access to over 5,000 books and videos, as well as industry leading tools to help you plan your personal development and advance your career. For more information, please visit our website.

Why subscribe?

- Spend less time learning and more time coding with practical eBooks and Videos from over 4,000 industry professionals

- Improve your learning with Skill Plans built especially for you

- Get a free eBook or video every month

- Mapt is fully searchable

- Copy and paste, print, and bookmark content

Packt.com

Did you know that Packt offers eBook versions of every book published, with PDF and ePub files available? You can upgrade to the eBook version at `www.packt.com` and as a print book customer, you are entitled to a discount on the eBook copy. Get in touch with us at `customercare@packtpub.com` for more details.

At `www.packt.com`, you can also read a collection of free technical articles, sign up for a range of free newsletters, and receive exclusive discounts and offers on Packt books and eBooks.

Contributors

About the author

Cesar Anton Dorantes has been a Google Developers Experts program member since 2013, being the first Mexican and second person in Latin America to receive the distinction. He is also among the first recognized Google Drive Experts worldwide. He is known for his rapid prototyping skills and passion for UX. A strong advocate of Google Design Sprint, he believes good ideas can be transformed into a product in days. As an architect, he prefers serverless cloud infrastructures, aiming for reliable solutions that can scale to millions of users. His experience includes working for one of Latin America's most recognized education start-ups, one of the US's largest media companies, and one of the world's largest software engineering providers.

I would like to thank my wife, Alejandra Jiménez, for her continuous support and motivation to write this book and keep pursuing our dreams; my parents for giving me the support and education that allowed me to become a professional; my best friend, Uriel Lara, for always believing in me and providing unconditional support; and all the people at Google who gave me the opportunity to prove myself and share my passion for technology with the world.

About the reviewer

Born in Zugdidi, Georgia, **Dima Sitchinava** showed a keen interest in technology from childhood. He was 15 when he finished schooling and enrolled himself at Georgian Technical University, where he graduated from the Information Technology Faculty. This was followed by a master's degree from Shota Meskhia State Teaching University. After his master's, he started working as a manager of computer laboratories at his alma mater. Having worked with a myriad of organizations, he currently works as a lecturer of vocational programs.

Packt is searching for authors like you

If you're interested in becoming an author for Packt, please visit authors.packtpub.com and apply today. We have worked with thousands of developers and tech professionals, just like you, to help them share their insight with the global tech community. You can make a general application, apply for a specific hot topic that we are recruiting an author for, or submit your own idea.

Table of Contents

Section 2: G Suite with Google Domains

Section 4: Apps and Sites

Preface

G Suite is a cloud-based office suite created by Google that allows businesses to operate without many of the complications associated with traditional software, such as the constant risk of data loss, and the requirement of a professional installation on each device. It also helps to mitigate security issues related to the storage and sharing of data on physical devices.

Welcome to *Hands-On G Suite for Administrators*, a comprehensive guide to G Suite administration that will get you started on your path to becoming a G Suite administrator, ready to handle all business scales, from a small office to a large enterprise.

You will start by learning the main features, tools, and services from G Suite for Business, and then you will explore all it has to offer, along with its best practices, so you can make the most out of G Suite for Business.

You will learn how to set up, analyze, and enforce security and privacy for your business and how to efficiently troubleshoot a wide variety of issues.

Finally, you will also learn how to use Google Sites to create beautiful websites that adapt to different screen sizes and can integrate with live documents and external services including Facebook and PayPal.

Who this book is for

This book is for aspirants to the Google Suite Administrator Certificate, system administrators, cloud administrators, and business professionals looking to learn how to effectively use and implement Google Suite tools and administration for business.

What this book covers

Chapter 1, *Getting Started with G Suite,* takes you through the steps for creating a G Suite for Business account and setting up the initial configuration.

Chapter 2, *Administering Gmail for Business,* shows you the steps you need to take to set up Gmail for Business and how to integrate it with existing services such as Microsoft Outlook.

Chapter 3, *Team Collaboration with G Suite*, teaches you how to make the best use of G Suite services, such as Calendar, Google Groups, private G+ communities, Hangouts, and Google Drive.

Chapter 4, *Moving On with Data Migration Services*, guides you through the steps and requirements for migrating emails, contacts, and calendar information from other services into G Suite.

Chapter 5, *Setting Up Domains and Users*, shows you the different options for adding additional domains so that your organization can associate multiple domains or keep them independent from each other, as well as how to administer user accounts across multiple domains.

Chapter 6, *Monitoring Reports*, guides you through the main reports provided by G Suite and what they can teach you about your organization.

Chapter 7, *Archiving with Vault*, demonstrates how to set up Vault to ensure you comply with legal requirements for issues related to virtually anything that happens in your G Suite domain by creating legal holds on specific information that is under investigation for potential legal issues.

Chapter 8, *Setting Up Security*, guides you through the configuration of the security features of G Suite according to your organization's requirements.

Chapter 9, *Getting Started with Google Sites*, teaches you how to create responsive websites using a collaborative platform that requires no coding skills.

To get the most out of this book

To get the most out of this book, follow the steps and create your own G Suite for Business account. I recommend you set yourself the goal of finishing this book within the 14-day free trial for new G Suite accounts.

You will require a computer with internet access and a valid credit card—you will not be charged during the free trial period.

To continue learning after you finish this book, visit Google's G Suite Administration training program at `cloud.google.com/training/admin`. Here, you will find the following:

- A link to a free self-study course that will help you reinforce what you've learned in this book through videos, quizzes, and hands-on exercises.
- A link to the *What's New for G Suite Admins* YouTube channel, where you can watch videos with monthly news and updates related to G Suite. Subscribe to this channel so that you are notified when a new video is released.

Download the color images

We also provide a PDF file that has color images of the screenshots/diagrams used in this book. You can download it here: `http://www.packtpub.com/sites/default/files/downloads/9781789613018_ColorImages.pdf`.

Conventions used

There are a number of text conventions used throughout this book.

`CodeInText`: Indicates code words in text, database table names, folder names, filenames, file extensions, pathnames, dummy URLs, user input, and Twitter handles. Here is an example: "Type the custom **Web Address** you want for this site—for example, `products.cesarstechinsight.net`."

Bold: Indicates a new term, an important word, or words that you see onscreen. For example, words in menus or dialog boxes appear in the text like this. Here is an example: "Confirm that **URL Format** is set to **new Sites**."

Warnings or important notes appear like this.

Tips and tricks appear like this.

Get in touch

Feedback from our readers is always welcome.

General feedback: If you have questions about any aspect of this book, mention the book title in the subject of your message and email us at customercare@packtpub.com.

Errata: Although we have taken every care to ensure the accuracy of our content, mistakes do happen. If you have found a mistake in this book, we would be grateful if you would report this to us. Please visit www.packt.com/submit-errata, selecting your book, clicking on the Errata Submission Form link, and entering the details.

Piracy: If you come across any illegal copies of our works in any form on the Internet, we would be grateful if you would provide us with the location address or website name. Please contact us at copyright@packt.com with a link to the material.

If you are interested in becoming an author: If there is a topic that you have expertise in and you are interested in either writing or contributing to a book, please visit authors.packtpub.com.

Reviews

Please leave a review. Once you have read and used this book, why not leave a review on the site that you purchased it from? Potential readers can then see and use your unbiased opinion to make purchase decisions, we at Packt can understand what you think about our products, and our authors can see your feedback on their book. Thank you!

For more information about Packt, please visit packt.com.

Section 1: G Suite for Business

1

In this section, you will learn about the initial configuration, how to use the main features and services of G Suite, and how to migrate from a previous corporate network.

The following chapters are included in this section:

- Chapter 1, *Getting Started with G Suite*
- Chapter 2, *Administering Gmail for Business*
- Chapter 3, *Team Collaboration with G Suite*
- Chapter 4, *Moving On with Data Migration Services*

Getting Started with G Suite 1

Computers are an essential tool for modern businesses, mostly due to the popularity of office suite software, which, since its invention back in the 1980s, has become so popular that virtually every office computer has one installed. Communication is also essential and it is hard to imagine a computer these days, especially inside an office, that doesn't have an internet connection to at least check emails.

There are some problems associated with traditional software though—mostly that it has to be individually installed and updated on every piece of equipment, and to collaborate on a single document, copies need to be sent back and forth, usually by email or via a physical device, which becomes a bigger problem as teams grow in size and complexity.

Google's G Suite for Business offers an alternative that runs directly in the internet browser, taking advantage of modern web languages and protocols. This means that there is no need to install or apply updates at all: with the simple combination of a username and password, users get instant access to a set of over 15 web services provided by Google. These services aim to cover the main needs of modern businesses in terms of communication and productivity, with a strong focus in collaboration, accessibility, and security. Even though many of Google's services are free for personal use, business accounts allow the use a custom domain, along with other features including advanced security and management, to better fit the needs of virtually any business.

In this chapter, you will learn how to do the following:

- Identifying the key features and advantages of G Suite
- Setting up a G Suite for Business account
- Adding basic customization to G Suite
- Configuring Contacts

Understanding G Suite

Google has embraced the post-PC era by allowing users to also access all services from mobile devices, such as phones, tablets, and other, newer formats, such as transformable and hybrid laptops and tablets. Being a web-based service, all that is needed is a device with a modern web browser and internet access. This flexibility not only makes things more convenient for the users, but also creates opportunities to cut costs on specialized hardware and the associated software maintenance. Setting up a new device can be as easy as opening the web browser and entering the username and password.

Windows is very common on the standard PC, but its license comes at a cost, and if, at the end of the day, we only need a browser and an office suite, we can cover those needs using one of Google's free operating systems: Android or Chrome OS. G Suite for Business seamlessly integrates with these operating systems, allowing you to set up a device you connected to the internet and log in using your corporate account, as well as boosting security, with features including remotely blocking or deleting a lost or stolen device. Everything is instantly available and all configurations are applied automatically. These devices are usually far cheaper, work surprisingly fast, and require little maintenance.

Collaboration is important for efficient teamwork, and G Suite allows teams to work together regardless of distance. Several users can work on a single document, presentation, or spreadsheet in real time. Teams can also chat or talk in video conferences, or even mix these options and create a document while talking, seeing each other, and sharing notes.

Real-time collaboration improves efficiency in tasks that can be done in parallel, but some projects can also benefit from having a team working in different time zones to allow the project to keep going continuously. Remote collaboration also enables the selection of the best of a wider range of candidates—there is no need to be limited to local talent.

G Suite is also very cost-effective for business. Savings increase as the number of users grows. Companies no longer have to worry about buying a license for every computer, and having to cover the installation, configuration, and maintenance costs for each device.

As a business grows, management becomes increasingly important and complex. You may be able to handle business with ease when there are only five or ten members, but when you need to administer hundreds or thousands of users, you really need a strong management system to keep things in check and running smoothly.

Keeping information safe can be hard when dealing with local files, as users could simply copy them to some external storage. To trace those operations, a business needs to use specially configured hardware and software, which not only costs more money, but also requires installation, license management, and maintenance. G Suite is secured by design—everything was built with a security-first approach with data encryption at every step; it doesn't rely on local files; and it comes with management and security features embedded at no extra cost.

File changes are saved in real time, so accidental data loss due to hardware or electric failures is no longer a problem. On top of this, all changes are recorded, and you can review and rollback to any previous state, and even review the people who made every change, including the day and time. Views, shares, downloads, prints, creations, and deletions are also stored, and can be audited at any time with ease.

When you enroll, Google gives you a 14-day free trial. This lets you get things started. At the time of this publication G Suite price is divided in three tiers: **Basic**, at USD $6, **Business**, at USD $12, and **Enterprise**, at USD $25. Prices work on a per-user-per-monthly basis, and the administration and security services are included. All tiers also benefit from 24/7 support by phone, email, and online.

Usually, businesses use the flexible billing plan, where you get charged every month based on the number of active users on your domain. Enterprise accounts can also choose an annual billing plan, where they commit to pay for a certain amount of licenses every month for a full year. It's possible to increase the number of licenses, but they can only be decreased when renewing the contract every year.

With the Basic account, you get 30 GB of storage for every user. Business and Enterprise accounts with four users or less get 1 TB of storage per account, and for five or more users, cloud storage is unlimited.

Business and Enterprise accounts also include low-code app development services for easy creation of corporate apps using templates, a drag-and-drop editor, and simplified data modeling. These accounts allow you to control how long emails, chats and messages are retained for all accounts in the domain to comply with data holding requirements in the case of a legal issue. Administrators can track all user activity and use **eDiscovery** to audit all email, chat, and file content for the entire company.

Enterprise accounts are best for handling large amounts of users, as they include the **Security Center**, which provides a unified security dashboard that allows administrators to quickly identify, triage, and take action against any security threat or suspicious activity. Enterprise accounts also benefit from advanced data loss prevention for Gmail and Google Drive, digitally signed and encrypted emails, the option to use a physical security key to login, Gmail log analysis via **BigQuery**, and the option to integrate Gmail with third-party archiving tools.

Setting up a G Suite for Business account

It's easy to set up a G Suite for Business account, but to make it as straightforward as possible, it's best to have a few things prepared before starting.

As a G Suite admin, the first thing you need is the name for your new business account, as it will be seen by the world. For example, I chose to use the name of my personal blog, *Cesar's Tech Insights*. You will also need the business address information and the credit card that will be used for the monthly payment. If you don't have a credit card on hand, you can still register the new account and set up billing later. Google will hold your account for about 10 days and you will receive a notice three days before the deadline, after which the account will be permanently deleted.

There will be no charges related to G Suite for the first 14 days, but if you buy a new custom domain, you will have to pay for it immediately. It is possible to use a previously existing domain, or to cancel G Suite but keep the domain.

The following are the steps required to create and register a G Suite for Business account:

1. Let's open a browser window, go to `gsuite.google.com`, and click on **GET STARTED** on the top right corner, as shown in the following screenshot:

2. Welcome to the **Let's get started** page. Here, you need to type a **Business name**, the **Number of employees, including you** within the organization and the main **Country** of operations. You can type your name as the **Business name** if this is a professional account. Click **NEXT** when you finish:

Business name

Number of employees, including you

○ Just you

○ 2-9

○ 10-99

○ 100-299

○ 300+

Country
United States

NEXT

3. On this step you need to provide your contact information for this account. Just type in your **First name, Last name**, and **Current email address**. Google will send the account information and next steps to this email. Click **NEXT** when you finish:

First name

Last name

Current email address

NEXT

4. In this step, you will select this account's domain, which will be used at the end of all accounts and any website. You will be asked if you already have a business domain or if you need one. For now, click **NO, I NEED ONE** to create a new one:

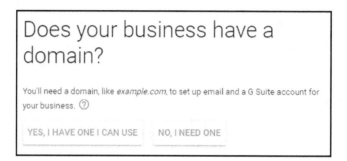

5. Type the address you would like in the search box and verify whether it's available:

6. Try looking for domains that match your business name. Keep in mind that some domains are more expensive than others. For example, I chose cesarstechinsights**.net** instead of cesarstechinsights**.com**, as .net domains are cheaper. Using a .co domain is a popular alternative with startups, since it still has plenty of available domains and it's shorter than .com, while remaining familiar. Once you've found the desired domain, click **NEXT** to proceed:

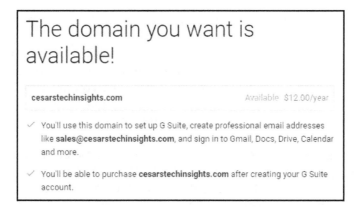

The domain you want is available!

cesarstechinsights.com   Available $12.00/year

✓ You'll use this domain to set up G Suite, create professional email addresses like **sales@cesarstechinsights.com**, and sign in to Gmail, Docs, Drive, Calendar and more.

✓ You'll be able to purchase **cesarstechinsights.com** after creating your G Suite account.

7. Now it's time to enter business information for the account. You will be asked to provide your address, city, country, ZIP code, and phone number. After filling all fields, click **NEXT** to go to the next step:

Enter your business information

Enter your business information to register your domain. ⑦

Street address

Street address line 2

City

State   ▾   ZIP code

Business phone number

8. To finish the G Suite account registration for our domain, we need to create an email for the administrator. I recommend using **admin**@businessDomain.com and a password of at least eight characters. Make sure to use a combination of upper and lowercase letters, and some special characters for added security. Before continuing, you must prove that you are not some automated software pretending to be a human. For this, click on the checkbox next to the **I'm not a robot** button. You may be asked to complete a simple challenge to prove you are human. Once you have provided the administrator's username and password, and completed the **reCAPTCHA** challenge, click on **AGREE AND CONTINUE** to finish the initial registration flow. If you are using the Chrome browser, **Google Smart Lock** will offer to remember the login credentials for you automatically:

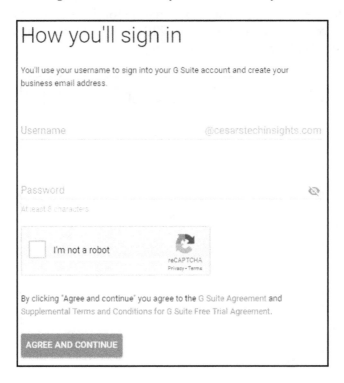

You can change the administrator email later to **yourName**@businessDomain.com and keep **admin**@businessDomain.com as an alias, which makes it easier for people to find you.

A **Welcome to your G Suite trial** email will be sent to the email you used at the setup process, containing the username, domain, subscription type, trial end date, a direct sign-in button, and a URL, which will be http://admin.google.com/ plus your custom domain. Click the **Sign In** button to begin your first sign-in. As a final confirmation step, you will be asked to validate your identity by providing a security code sent to you through the phone number you registered. You can choose to receive a voice call or an SMS message. Pick the one that you prefer and input the code to finish the validation process. You will see a **Welcome to your new account** message, containing a summary of the terms and conditions, with some links to places were you can read more details. After you finish reading and understanding them, click the **Accept** button to finish the initial setup and go the G Suite administrator's home for the new account.

Before we start using the new account, click on the Billing icon to set up payments. If you didn't sign up for G Suite Enterprise, you will be able to choose from G Suite Business or Basic editions. Choose the one that best suits your business needs. Here, you should choose the billing country and currency. This will affect your payment options and you will not be able to change this information later. The payment methods vary from country to country. The most common way is to use a Visa, MasterCard, or American Express card, but in some countries it's also possible to link it directly to your bank account.

Congratulations! Your G Suite for Business account is now fully active. Remember, there will be no charges until the end of your trial period.

Customizing G Suite

Showing the organization's name and logo on the corporate web software, gives a more professional look and also helps members identify themselves as part of it.

G Suite for Business allows you to personalize its look and behavior to match your business style, needs, and preferences. To change the general settings, go to the **Administrator Home** and click on **Company profile:**

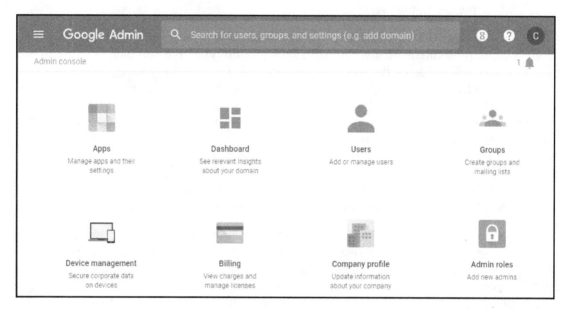

You are now ready to start setting up this new domain. In the next section, you will learn how to set up the **Company profile**.

Profile

The **Company profile** holds the organization's general information and preferences, and it's your first step into personalizing G Suite.

In this section, we'll set up the basic company information and some preferences. Let's explore them in detail:

- **Organization name:** This field will be used in all your Google services and public information for this account. This will be the same for all the domains that are registered for this G Suite account.
- **Contact information:** You will see the administrators contact emails.
  The primary administrator account is the email for this domain where users can reach you, and the secondary email address is the personal email you used for the registration flow.

- **Support message**: This message is shown to users who are looking for help information about the domain. This is some additional information that you wish to tell your users when they are looking for help; for example, your service hours and any other relevant information.
- **Language**: This field sets the default language for new accounts in this domain. Individual users may set up their own language preferences later.
- **Time zone**: This section has two drop-down menus that allows you to define a default time zone:
    - The first is used to narrow down the list of time zones to those that are within a country
    - The second is used to actually select the time zone you wish to apply as default
- **New user features**: Google Suite is a continuously evolving platform, and updates are released constantly. In the new user features release policy, you can choose when those changes will be applied to your team's workspace. For this, you have two options: **Rapid release**, which means you want newly released features to be applied immediately for your team, and **Scheduled release,** which allows you to hold any changes for some time so you can learn about the changes and prepare your team in advance. This is usually one or two weeks after the actual release.
- **New products**: Here, we have a new products release policy, where you can choose when you prefer to make new G Suite products available for your team. You can choose for them to be released according to an **Automatic** policy, which will make new products immediately available, or the **Manual** policy, which will notify the administrator of new products and leave it up to you if and when they will be made available for the team.
- **Analytics**: This option allows you to activate tracking of the use of Google services from this account. We will come back to this in another chapter.
- **Account deletion**: This section holds the requirements and a button to permanently delete this account. However, before doing so, it will require you to cancel all active payment subscriptions. If you bought the domain name through Google, it will also ask you to transfer it before the **Delete this account** option becomes available.
- **Security and privacy additional terms**: This section contains a list with a few amendments for you to review and agree to, if they are applicable to your needs. Please review them carefully by clicking on each one, then press **REVIEW AND ACCEPT** on the ones that apply to your account.

Click **SAVE** on the bottom right to save any changes you made to the **Company Profile**. You can come back to this section in the future to update these settings.

Now that you know how to set up the general information and preferences for this domain, let's continue to the next section to learn what **Communication preferences** are and how to define them.

Communication preferences

Google likes keeping in touch and helping it's business clients—that applies to all G Suite accounts—regardless of how many members are in the organization.

In **Communication preferences**, you will tell Google what kind of notifications you would be interested in being sent to you via email. By default, they are all enabled. Let's explore the options here:

- **Performance suggestions and updates** will send you updates on G Suite services, along with various tips and resources to learn more about Google Cloud
- **Feature announcements** will send you details related to changes, improvements, and new features being released on G Suite
- **Offers from Google** will keep you updated about product launches, Google events, and special promotions
- **Feedback and testing** will allow you to participate in service surveys, as well as giving you the option to join pilot programs to allow your team to help shape the future of G Suite

Defining your communication preferences was a breeze—let's continue to the next section and learn what we can do with **Personalization**.

Personalization

Here, you can upload your company logo, which will replace the current Google logo in all products used through this account. Click on **CHOOSE FILE** to find the image you want to use on your current device local storage, and then click on **UPLOAD** to apply it:

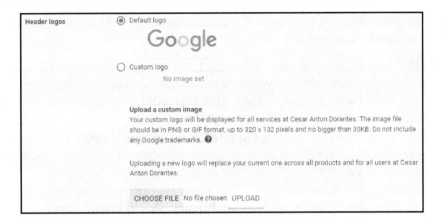

Now you know where to go when you need to change the logo of the domain.

Supplemental data storage

This section allows you to store a copy of some or all of the users' data in servers located in the country you select, acting as a redundant copy of the standard **Google Datastore**.

To activate this option, select any of the countries you see on the list and click **Save**. Keep in mind that this may take up to 24 hours to be applied to all the users in this domain. Once you have organizational units, you can use them to limit the scope of the supplemental data storage.

At the moment of writing this, the only option is the Russian Federation. This was a response from Google in 2015 to comply with a law requiring internet companies to store Russian's data within the country, so if your organization is based in Russia, you might be legally required to use this option.

This is a very specific case of legal compliance. In the next section, we will learn how to set up more common **Legal and compliance** settings.

Legal and compliance

As an administrator, you might be required to help providing data to support some legal issue or to hold data copies in specific way to comply with legal requirements.

In this section, you can find a list of useful resources that will help you fulfill your legal requirements.

The various options you have relating to the legal issues and regulatory compliance for your G Suite account are as follows:

1. In this section, the first element on the list will be **Google Cloud Storage Locations**, which will take you to a site where you will be able to see the locations of Google's data centers. This is worth looking at if your business is sensitive about the physical location of your data.

2. The second item on the list is **Google Cloud subprocessors**. This refers to a list of Google affiliates that help the company with some of their services, such as customer support and hiring agreements.

3. The third section contains the current **Private certifications** that G Suite has from other third parties, such as the **Privacy Shield Framework**.

4. The fourth section refers to **Security certifications and third-party audits**, which shows more details on all the certifications, standards, and regulations that Google Cloud keeps in compliance with.

5. Next, we have the **Google security overview**, which has a link to download the **Google Cloud security white paper** that explains all the security features and certifications of Google Cloud.

6. Then, we have **Google's cloud data protection team**, which offers a direct link to the **G Suite Administrator Help**. This contains an FAQ of common problems, as well as instructions on what to do before asking for support and how to get it.

7. Finally, you will find fields that, if applicable, you should fill with the contact information of your business **EU representative** and the **data protection officer**, which is a **General Data Protection Regulation** (**GDPR**) requirement for businesses in the European Union.

Hopefully, you won't be needing this much. Let's continue with our legal compliance by learning how **Data regions** can help us meet physical requirements for digital data in G Suite.

Data regions

If your business data is location-sensitive due to legal reasons, and your G Suite account is registered under the Business, Educational, or Enterprise edition, then you can use this section to ask Google to keep the team's Gmail, Calendar, Drive, Hangouts Chat, Docs, Sheets, Slides, and Vault stored in a specific geographic location in the U.S. or Europe. Do keep in mind that if any of your users needs access to any of this content outside the selected region, then they might experience slower loading speeds and higher latency, impacting mostly the real-time services:

Data regions policy Locally applied	Set a policy for where you want to store covered data for the selected organizational unit.
	⚠ Enabling this policy involves making performance tradeoffs. Learn more
	ⓘ Data regions policies cover only certain Core Services' data. Learn more
	◉ No preference
	○ United States
	○ Europe

And now you have the basic legal compliance settings covered for this domain. Let's continue to the next section to learn how to use **Custom URLs** for the different G Suite services in this organization.

Custom URLs

This section allows your team to access G Suite using custom URLs for Gmail, Calendar, Drive, Sites, and Groups for Business under the company's domain, instead of the default ones, making it much easier to remember. For example, the *Cesar's Tech Insights* team can access Gmail through `http://mail.cesarstechinsights.net`, instead of the default `https://mail.google.com/a/cesarstechinsights.net`, which is much harder to remember:

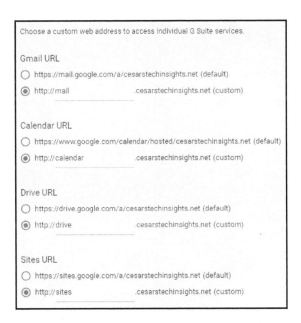

For this section, just enter the alias you want to use for each one of the services and click **Save**.

You can now set up a company profile—we are just getting started. In the next section, we will how **G Suite Contacts** can help our organization and how to set it up.

Setting up G Suite Contacts

Business usually don't work in isolation—they need to keep in contact with clients, suppliers, associates, partners, and so on. This can be easy to coordinate at first, but as the business grows, keeping an updated and safe corporate directory becomes increasingly complex.

G Suite Contacts allows your team to keep a shared global directory to find and maintain relevant business contact information.

Let's go to the **Directory** and set the contact sharing options for your team from the administrator home, as follows:

1. Click on the Main menu icon
2. Hover over **Directory**
3. Lastly, click **Sharing settings**, and you should see the following:

Sharing settings

Decide how users can share contacts, both within your organization and externally

---

You will see a list of options. Let's explore what they do in the following sections.

Contact Sharing

First, you will have the option to enable or disable contact sharing. When enabled, the contacts list will be shared automatically across your team so everyone can create, access, and update the team's sharing.

Here, you can also choose how much information will be shared in the **Global directory**. To make all information shared, choose **Show all email addresses** to make all emails, both personal and business available for everyone. With **Show both domain profiles and domain shared contacts**; **domain profiles** refers to the team members' contact information, and **shared contacts** refers to information about people who are not part of the team:

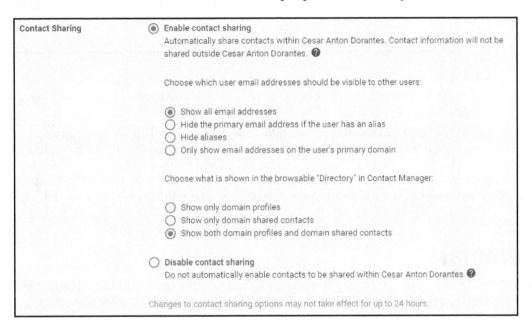

Click **Save** to apply changes. Keep in mind that this may take up to 24 hours to take effect for the entire team.

External Directory Sharing

It is very common to integrate a G Suite account with third-party applications. Here, you control how much of the team's global directory will be available to these external apps:

External Directory Sharing	○ Only public data
	Share domain profile data that has public visibility with external apps and APIs. By default all domain data should have domain visibility and so will not be shared ❓
	⦿ Domain and public data
	Share domain shared contacts data and domain profile data that has domain or public visibility with external apps and APIs ❓
	Changes to contact sharing options may not take effect for up to 24 hours.

- **Only public data** will only allow third-party apps to access information that is already available to the public. This will not include contacts' information stored in the directory.
- **Domain and public data** is the default setting and will allow external apps to access all information stored in the directory, as well as the already-public data.

Now you know how to set up G Suite Contacts, and with that, we conclude this chapter. But before we continue, let's take a moment to review all the things we just learned.

Summary

In this chapter, we learned the key features of G Suite for Business and the advantages of using web-based software over the traditional approach of installing software on each machine.

We also learned how G Suite helps your team to be more productive through secure, real-time collaboration, maximizing productivity while keeping costs down and scaling with team growth, from small start-ups to large enterprises.

You are now able to identify the different pricing and storage options, estimate costs, and choose the right plan for your team, regardless of size and complexity.

Now you can create a new account, find and set up a new domain, personalize it, and configure a shared global directory.

Now that you know how to create a new domain, the next thing you need to learn is how to set up a business email service. We will cover all the details for that and more in Chapter 2, *Administering Gmail for Business*.

In Chapter 5, *Setting Up Domains and Users*, we will go deeper into the configurations for this domain and how to add more than one domain.

2
Administering Gmail for Business

Starting off with Gmail, today's business version of G Suite is very robust and has become an integral cog of corporate machinery. Since email is the primary mode of communication with clients, partners, and providers, ensuring its security is the need of the hour.

Sending emails should be a simple task for users, but from an administration point of view, there are many things to do and maintain in order to keep emails that are coming and going safe and without problems.

Sending and reading emails should be easy and intuitive, and, as a G Suite administrator, one of your duties is to ensure that things are fine-tuned to your organization's particular needs. Gmail for Business offers several options that allow you to do that. In this chapter, we will explore all the different settings so that you can choose the correct combination for your team.

To get you ready for your Gmail duties as a G Suite administrator, in this chapter, you will learn the following topics:

- How to configure Gmail for Business
- Allowing other users within the team to access your account
- Controlling spam
- Identifying and setting up security features and standards in G Suite
- Integrating with Microsoft Outlook
- How to send email to groups of users

In the upcoming pages we will explore the main G Suite configurations as we find them on **Admin Home**. Let's begin our quest of understanding Gmail for Business from the G Suite administrator's point of view.

Understanding Gmail for Business

Gmail for Business offers ample storage for your team. If there are fewer than five members, each one gets 1 TB, but once the team grows, the unlimited storage option will be automatically enabled.

There are some limitations as regards messages. The most common one is that outbound email attachments are limited to 25 MB, while inbound attachments can only be up to 50 MB in size for a single message. Other usually less relevant restrictions are that your team can only send a single message to up to 500 addresses, and users can only send up to 3,000 messages per day outside of your domain.

To find Gmail settings, take these steps from the administrator home:

1. Select **Apps**
2. Click on **G Suite**
3. Select **Gmail**

You will be taken to the **Settings for Gmail** main screen. Here, you will find several expansion panels, each one holding one type of configuration:

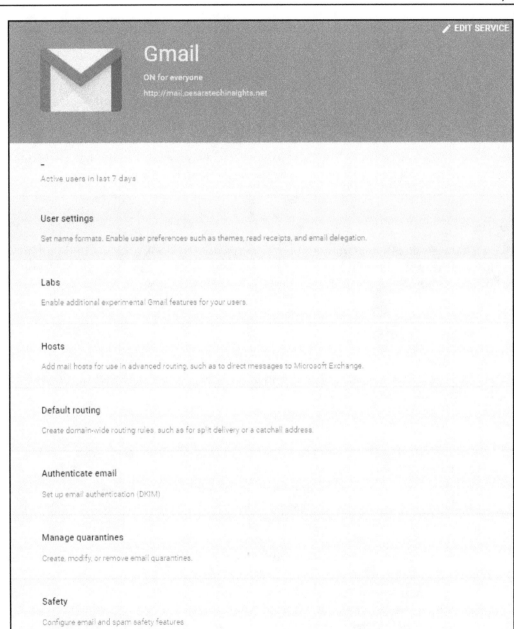

EDIT SERVICE

Gmail

ON for everyone

http://mail.cesarstechinsights.net

-

Active users in last 7 days

User settings

Set name formats. Enable user preferences such as themes, read receipts, and email delegation.

Labs

Enable additional experimental Gmail features for your users.

Hosts

Add mail hosts for use in advanced routing, such as to direct messages to Microsoft Exchange.

Default routing

Create domain-wide routing rules, such as for split delivery or a catchall address.

Authenticate email

Set up email authentication (DKIM)

Manage quarantines

Create, modify, or remove email quarantines.

Safety

Configure email and spam safety features

Advanced settings »

Access other settings for controlling mail flow for the domain.

To define a configuration, click on a panel to unfold its contents. After making changes, click **SAVE** to apply them.

Let's start our configuration at the top of the list with **User settings**.

Setting up default user settings

While creating a new account, it is a good idea to start by configuring the **User settings** to define the general look and control the options available to the domain's team.

Themes

Enabling **Themes** will allow team members to customize the look and feel of their Gmail accounts, while disabling it will force everyone to keep the default appearance. Users cannot hide the company logo and their settings will only be applied to their accounts.

Email Read Receipts

Gmail for Business offers the option to verify whether an email has been read by the recipient. As a G Suite administrator, you can make this possible by enabling **Email Read Receipts** in the domain accounts.

During configuration, you will see the following options:

- **Do not allow read receipts to be sent**: This option disables the use of read receipts within the domain.
- **Allow email read receipts to be sent to all addresses in my organization as well as the following email addresses**: This option will restrict read receipts to be used only internally with the addition of up to 100 external emails. Once enabled, you can write the external addresses allowed by separating them with a comma. There is also an option to manually confirm with the user when there is a read receipt or if they should be sent automatically.
- **Allow email read receipts to be sent to any email address**: This will enable read receipts for all internal and external email addresses, but will confirm with the user every time there is such request. These options are demonstrated in the following screenshot:

Email Read Receipts
Locally applied

Read receipts are notifications that can be sent to and from your users to verify that mail has been read. ❷

◯ Do not allow email read receipts to be sent.

◯ Allow email read receipts to be sent to all addresses in my organization as well as the following email addresses:

_____

Enter comma separated email addresses to allow read receipts to be sent to. Maximum of 100 entries of up to 256 characters each.

☑ Prompt the user for each read receipt request.
Email read receipts are automatically sent unless this option is selected.

◉ Allow email read receipts to be sent to any email address.
Users will be prompted each time a read receipt is requested.

Now that your users can use email read receipts to confirm that someone read an important message it's time to learn how **Mail Delegation** can help users during their vacations.

Mail Delegation

There are cases where someone in the team wants to delegate access to their personal inbox to other members of the organization. This is very useful when a key member of staff is on vacation or has an assistant. **Mail Delegation** gives the option to share access to the corporate inbox in a secure way, since all actions will be recorded and can be audited in the future if required.

Delegates can only be added or removed from the web. The app version doesn't provide this option.

Adding a delegate

Once **Mail Delegation** is enabled, each user can add up to 25 delegates. To do this, they should go to their Gmail for Business inbox, click **Settings** ⚙ in the top-right corner, and then click **Settings**:

Go to the **Accounts** tab and look for the **Grant access to your account** section and select whether you wish to mark conversations as read when one of your delegates has read it, or only when you have read them yourself:

To add a new delegate, we need to observe the following steps:

1. Click on **Add another account.**
2. Write the email of the person within your organization to whom you wish to grant access.
3. Click **Next Step:**

4. Click **Send email to grant access** in order to send the invitation to your colleague:

This will send an invitation where they can **Confirm** or **Reject** your invitation. Keep in mind that invitations expire if there is no confirmation within a week:

The email will take your colleague to a **Confirmation** window. Once the delegate clicks **Confirm**, it may take up to 24 hours to get processed, so it's important to add delegates in sufficient time:

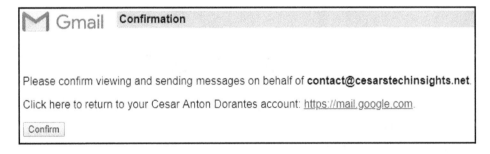

Removing a delegate

In the **Grant access to your account** section, you will see a list of emails with access to your account. If you wish to remove one of them, simply hover over the email and click the **delete** sign next to it:

You can now tell your users how to grant or remove access to their accounts while they are on scheduled time off.

Depending on where the organization is based the users might prefer different naming conventions, in the next section we will explore how to adjust this.

Name format

In **Name format,** you can choose whether people should be referred to by their first or last name at Gmail by default. If desired, users can choose to change this for their accounts.

This setting in not applied to names written in Chinese, Japanese, or Korean so members from these countries don't need to worry about their names being scrambled.

Gmail web offline

Gmail has the ability to use a technology called **service workers** that allows the site to work on the browser even when internet access is limited or non-existent. Enabling **Gmail web offline** will allow the members of this organization to use this feature from browsers.

Having this enabled is highly advisable because it will enhance the experience for your users and will prove particularly useful when having any kind of connectivity problem or limitation.

Enabling **Force deletion of offline data on sign out of Google account** is also recommended. This will erase all the information stored on the device when they log off, so they don't need to worry about cleaning the cache or leaving sensitive information:

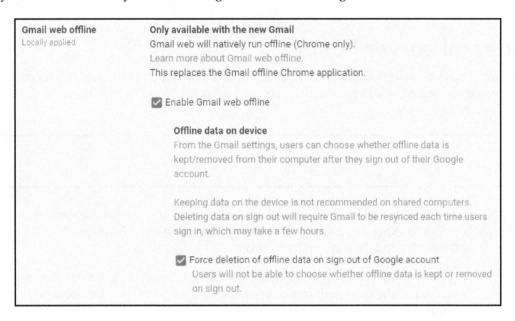

Being able to use Gmail offline without the need of installing any app makes things easier for your users when on the go, it allows them to use their commute time to read emails or work on drafts even when data is not reliable, such as when using the subway.

Enabling Labs

Gmail is testing out new features all the time, where you can allow members of your team to try experimental new features.

With **Labs** enabled, the newest features will be automatically available as soon as they are released:

You can also use **Advanced Labs Management** to manage features individually. Each lab will include a description of what it can do, and you can enable or disable them individually to keep a curated list of labs:

External server hosts

In **Hosts**, you can configure routes to external email servers such as Microsoft Exchange, or review your existing ones. In this section, you can see a list of all the active routes, edit them, or add new ones:

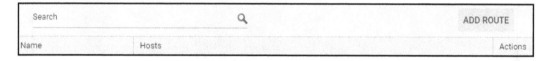

To add a new route, click **ADD ROUTE** and start by writing a name for this host. In the first section, select whether this route will be using a **Single host** or **Multiple hosts**, and then hostnames or IPs and their respective sockets.

Finally, let's select the **Options** you need. You can enable **Perform MX lookup on host** if you wish Gmail to use the mail exchange record and deliver to the hosts associated with the domain name:

If you are using multiple hosts, you can divide them into one or many **Primary** and **Secondary** routes, and even assign the load you wish to be routed to each one:

Setting up routes in a centralized place will make it easier for you to apply them later to define rules and services that works with external servers.

Setting up default email routing

When dealing with larger teams, it becomes increasingly necessary to be able to detect specific kinds of messages that need to be treated in some special way.

Default routing rules allows you to distribute, modify, or reject messages more efficiently across the domain depending on their characteristics. Here, you can see the rules that are currently active and quickly disable or delete existing rules or add a new one:

To add a new routing rule, select **ADD SETTING** and you will see a few options that will describe this new rule. Now, let's explore them.

Specify envelope recipients to match

In the first section, you can choose how you want to **Specify envelope recipients to match** for this new rule:

- **Single recipient**: Filter messages directed to a specific address from your domain.
- **Pattern match**: Detect messages that match a specific pattern in your domain.
- **Group membership**: Messages directed to one of the groups in this domain.
- **All recipients**: All incoming messages to unknown addresses. This is great for catching emails sent to an incorrect address inside your domain.

If the envelope recipient matches

Now that you have defined the envelope recipients that should be targeted with this rule, in this section, you have to define whether it should be rejected or allowed with modifications.

Modify message

In this part, you can see some of the options for modifying, tagging, or rerouting the message:

- **Headers**: A few selectable options of some pre-generated messages to the header or to create a custom one.
- **Subject**: Prepend a specific message to the subject.
- **Route**: Add this message to the normal route or a custom one.
- **Envelope recipient**: To change the recipient of the messages, equivalent to forwarding a copy of the message. When using this option, it's a good idea to also keep a copy of the original intended recipient using the custom headers.
- **Spam**: This will make this route accept emails tagged as spam.
- **Attachments**: Select this to remove attachments (highly recommended in most cases).
- **Also deliver to**:
    - **Normal**: Send a copy of the messages to a specific address. You can also use group addresses for this.
    - **Advanced**: This will allow you to send a copy using a custom route to create a sub-routing rule.

Reject message

You can add an optional rejection notice for the sender of this message. Simply fill the text field with the reply you wish to be sent to rejected messages:

We are almost finished adding a new route; our last step is to define the **Options** for this rule.

Options

The **Options** section allows you to define when this rule will apply:

- **Perform this action only on non-recognized addresses**: This will only apply this rule to unknown senders
- **Perform this action on non-recognized and recognized addresses**: This will apply this rule to all senders

You can now define default email routes for messages that matches specific criteria. This will allow you to automate tasks that otherwise would have to be done manually by users or administrators.

Setting up email authentication

As an administrator, one of your main tasks is keeping security tight, and Gmail for Business gives you the option to enhance the security of outgoing emails against spoofing by adding digital signatures based on the **DomainKeys Identified Mail** (**DKIM**) standard.

If you bought a domain through Google during the initial setup, the console will give you the option to automatically apply the required configuration to enable digital signatures. Simply click **START AUTHENTICATION** and, in a few seconds, everything will be ready.

In case you are using a third-party domain service, you can select **I'd rather configure the domain myself** and then click **Generate new record**, which will open a dialog allowing you to select the **DKIM key bit length** and an optional prefix used to distinguish this key from others that may be stored in the domain. After selecting your preferences, click **GENERATE** to get a TXT record name and a TXT record value that you will have to copy to your domain server.

Managing email quarantines

Gmail for Business allows you to **Manage quarantines** for inbound and outbound messages to prevent users from sending or clicking on something that may compromise security. Here, you can also designate users to manage the quarantined messages:

		GO TO ADMIN QUARANTINE	ADD QUARANTINE
Name	Description	Actions	

To define a new quarantine criterion, click **ADD QUARANTINE**. To add a quarantine, you are required to provide the following options:

- A **Name** for this quarantine
- A short **Description** of its purpose
- One or more **Quarantine reviewers group** that will help the **super admins** keep an eye on the messages that fall into it:

Name   Help

Description

Quarantine reviewers group ❓   Manage Groups

Select groups
If a group is not set or does not exist, then only super admins or delegated admins with
privilege "Access Admin Quarantine" can review the quarantine

- The **Inbound denial consequence** section allows you to define what happens when this rule matches incoming messages:
  - Select **Drop message** to ignore the messages
  - Select **Send the default reject message** to notify the sender that the message was rejected
- The **Outbound denial consequence** section allows you to define what happens for messages sent from the organization to external users:
  - Select **Drop message** to ignore the messages
  - Select **Send the default reject message** to notify the sender that the message was rejected

- Optionally, you can choose to **Notify periodically when messages are quarantined** so the administrator gets reports regarding quarantined messages:

Inbound denial consequence
○ Drop message
◉ Send the default reject message

Outbound denial consequence
○ Drop message
◉ Send the default reject message

☐ Notify periodically when messages are quarantined ❓

It may take several minutes for changes to propagate.

Finally, click **SAVE** to add the new quarantine. Once it's created, you can always come to **Manage quarantines** to **Edit** or **Delete** each criteria:

		GO TO ADMIN QUARANTINE	ADD QUARANTINE
Name	Description	Actions	
Default		Edit	
Example criteria 1	First example	Edit - Delete	
Example criteria 2	Second example	Edit - Delete	

Quarantines will allow you to deal with unwanted or dangerous messages in a centralized dashboard so it can be efficiently used even on large organizations.

You might have noticed that there are no specific rules associated at this point to our new quarantines, we will be using them as the final destination for other security rules.

This means that you will be able to associate the same quarantine to different rules; for example, you can make different rules to target phishing and make them all route messages to a single quarantine.

Admin Quarantine

All emails that match the criteria for quarantine will be sent here so that the admins and super admins can classify and choose the appropriate action. It's recommended to adjust the safety settings so that all suspicious email is sent here:

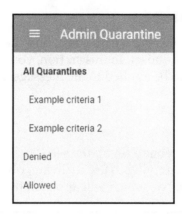

All newly quarantined messages will land in the **All Quarantines** tab. Super admins can create sub-categories for better manual classification using **Manage quarantines**.

If you are using Chrome, you can create app-like direct access for this (or any other) part of the G Suite admin console by clicking ⋮ in the top-right corner of the browser, and then **More tools**, followed by **Create shortcut**, and changing the default name if you wish. Make sure that you have **Open as window** activated and then click **Create**:

Once an action is taken against a quarantined message, it will be filed either as **Denied** or **Allowed**. This will simplify the auditing and double-checking of security decisions and apply corrections if needed.

Defining safety rules

Safety has the highest priority in Gmail for Business, and the team plans and builds everything with a security-first mindset. In this section, you will learn how to control the security features and behavior to be applied to the messages.

Attachments

The **Attachments** section allows you to set up the security settings that will protect the team from malicious third parties trying to use malware, phishing, or spoofing. By default, **Enable all settings** is active, which will apply all the rules with the default settings:

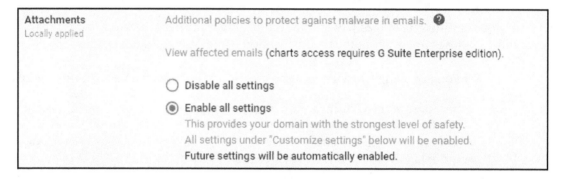

- **Disable all settings.** Choosing this will turn off attachment security. This is not recommended, even if you have an external attachment security service.

- **Customize settings.** It is recommended to use this option instead of **Enable all settings** since, with this option, you can **Choose an action** to have control of what will happen to messages that are targeted by this rule. By default, Gmail will just show a warning regarding suspicious messages, but you can also choose to **Move email to spam** so that it can be checked manually if necessary:

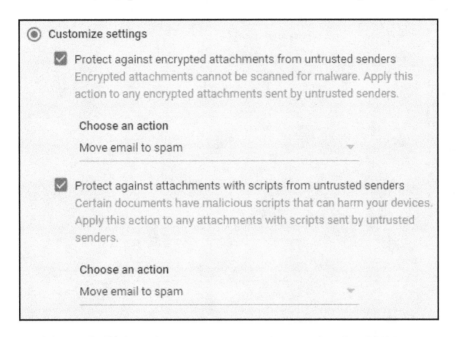

Attachments that are suspected of containing malware will be kept in the inbox and simply show a warning by default. I recommend changing this to **Move email to spam** instead so that an administrator can choose whether the email should be deleted or allowed to be seen by the intended recipient.

Links and external images

In **Links and external images**, you can define security rules that will be applied to links and images inside received messages in order to protect your team from phishing attempts:

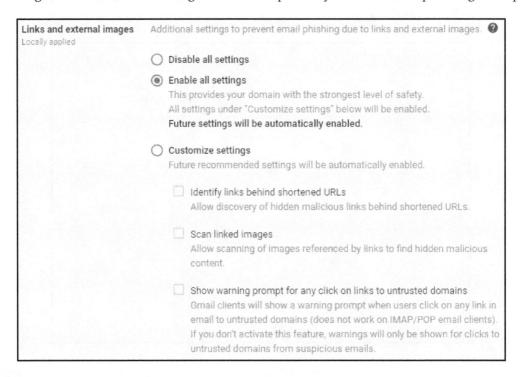

Most of the time, you should select **Enable all settings** to enable all the security features and get new ones enabled as soon as they become available. **Disable all settings** is usually only used when you are using a third-party service to handle your inbound security.

You can also choose to **Customize settings** and select just the measures you are interested in. If you enable **Identify links behind shortened URLs**, Google will look where they would take the user to identify malicious content, while **Scan linked images** will analyze images and try to identify malicious content.

You can also choose to **Show warning prompt for any click on links to untrusted domains** to warn users every time they try to click on links that would take them to any non-whitelisted domain.

Spoofing and authentication

Sometimes, we get messages that attempt to trick us into providing sensitive information by pretending to be a trusted source. This is a very common and effective way to tricking members of the organization into leaking data or providing their credentials:

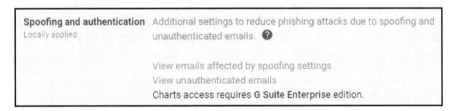

Spoofing and authentication contains several measures to keep the team protected:

- **Protect against domain spoofing based on similar domain names**: A common way to try to trick you into giving your password is showing you a fake login using a similar domain name. This option will make Gmail try to detect this kind of attack. You can choose whether it would be best to just show a warning next to suspicious messages or whether they should be moved to the spam folder directly:

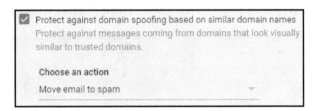

- **Protect against spoofing of employee names**: Enabling this will block messages coming from a known address, but which lacks the appropriate certificate. By default, it will keep the message and warn the user that the sender could not be confirmed, but it can be changed to **Move email to spam** instead so that it can be seen by the user if necessary:

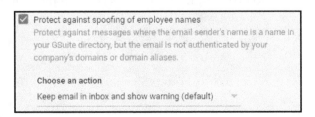

- **Protect against inbound emails spoofing your domain**: Attackers may attempt to steal information by sending messages using your domain as the origin. These may have a valid address from one of the members of the organization, but it will be lacking a digital certificate. In this section, you can choose how you wish to deal with these kinds of messages within your organization.
  By default, a warning will be shown to users before they open these kinds of messages, but they will be visible from their inbox. As an administrator, you can choose to change this to **Move email to spam** when they lack the proper certificate:

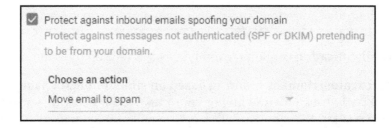

- **Protect against any unauthenticated emails.**This option will target all messages whose sender could not be verified. Usually, this has no action by default. But it's recommended to change it to **Move email to spam** or to **Keep email in inbox and show a warning** to warn the user of suspicious content:

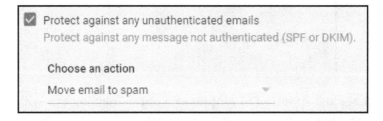

It's recommended to use an attack simulator for Gmail at random intervals to train your users into recognizing and acting against different kinds of phishing attacks.

Once or twice a month should be enough to keep everyone on the lookout for this kind of threat.

Exploring Advanced settings

Now that we have our general settings ready, it's time to go deeper and fine-tune all the details to keep messages flowing the way we want them to:

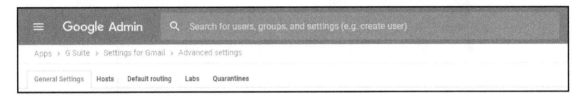

Advanced settings will redirect you to a dedicated dashboard to control the flow of emails, third-party integration, or disable Gmail for when you wish to use a third-party or private server for email purposes.

Notice that **Labs** and **Quarantines** are also accessible from this view and have the same features we saw in **Manage quarantines**, but they are also here for convenience.

Setup

Let's learn how to to set up the high-level details, such as the web address to access Gmail or even disable it completely.

Web address

Here, we can check the current address that members of the organization will be using to access Gmail. Remember that, by default, it comes with an ugly mail.google.com and here, you can change it to something like **mail**.yourdomain.co. To do so, click **Change URL** and you will be taken to the **Profile** dashboard, then click **Custom URLs**, and choose the custom alias you want to use within your domain for email access:

Web address	Your users can access Gmail at:
Locally applied	https://mail.google.com/a/cesarstechinsights.net
	Change URL

MX Records

You can also check the **Mail eXchanger** (**MX**) records, which is a list of the mailing servers linked to this account and their priority:

MX Records Locally applied	Your current MX records for cesarstechinsights.net:	
	Priority	Points to
	1	ASPMX.L.GOOGLE.COM.
	5	ALT1.ASPMX.L.GOOGLE.COM.
	5	ALT2.ASPMX.L.GOOGLE.COM.
	10	ASPMX2.GOOGLEMAIL.COM.
	10	ASPMX3.GOOGLEMAIL.COM.
	MX setup instructions	

If you haven't yet verified this domain, you can click on **MX setup instructions** to run the **G Suite Setup Wizard**, which will guide you to the proper instructions, depending on the domain host you are using.

User email uploads

Enabling **User email uploads** will allow members of your domain to use ShuttleCloud to import emails and contacts from previous accounts from Yahoo!, Hotmail, AOL, and also webmail and POP3 mailing services. This will greatly simplify migrating email accounts for your team if needed.

At the moment, ShuttleCloud is the only officially supported option to import emails from previous accounts:

User email uploads Locally applied	☐ Show users the option to import mail and contacts from Yahoo!, Hotmail, AOL, or other webmail or POP3 accounts from the Gmail settings page ❓ Importing is powered by ShuttleCloud. By selecting this checkbox, you agree to their Terms of Use and Privacy Policy. During import, the connection to the service provider may be unencrypted.

Uninstall service

Finally, you will see the option to uninstall the Gmail service, which you might need if the business has a private server with its own portal. Google will store any messages that your team had before disabling Gmail, and things can be restored by re-enabling it:

Uninstall service	Uninstall Gmail You can uninstall and remove this service without losing any data.

End User Access

Here, you can choose which of the available access options you wish to enable for the team:

- **POP and IMAP access**: If your team needs access to desktop clients such as Microsoft Outlook, you need to keep **POP and IMAP access** enabled, otherwise you can disable it here to increase security:

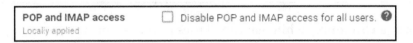

- **G Suite Sync**: This is a downloadable plugin that allows your team to integrate the Gmail service with Microsoft Outlook so as to keep contacts, calendar, emails, and even user status synchronized so that your team can keep using Outlook with G Suite:

- **Automatic forwarding**: Enable this to allow your team to forward messages automatically. In other words, it will hide the forward icon in Gmail:

- **Gmail Offline Chrome plugin**: Gmail can also work offline to read already-loaded emails or work on drafts. Enable this option to allow the team to use Gmail in these conditions.
  If this option is enabled, it is important to tell users to be extra careful and avoid using public or shared devices to access their Gmail account. In case they need to do so in an emergency, it is recommended to use an incognito or private browsing window and make sure to close it after they are done:

- **Allow per-user outbound gateways**: This will allow users to send emails through an external SMTP server and make it appear as if they are coming from your domain. Bear in mind that these messages will also bypass your outbound security:

- **Image URL proxy whitelist**: Gmail uses proxy servers to send images within messages in a secure way. Here, you can set up rules for images you wish to be allowed to bypass image security filters.
  To whitelist image URL routes, write them on the first line. The second line will allow you to test a specific image in order to confirm:

Image URL proxy whitelist	
Locally applied	Enter image URL patterns. Matching URLs bypass the image proxy. ❷
	Example: https://example.com/images
	Enter an image URL to preview. ❷
	Example: http://example.com/images/foo.jpg PREVIEW

- **Unintended external reply warning**: Business emails are usually sent to a large number of people and in message chains. New users can be added to the message at any point in the chain and, when replying to everyone, a member of your team can end up sending sensitive information to external users without noticing.
  Enabling this option will show a warning when replying to a message if a copy will be sent to someone the user has never contacted before and is not on their mailing list:

Now that you know how to define the options available for the members of the organization, in the next section we will explore spam settings.

Spam

Gmail for Business offers very strict spam filters, especially if you are using the recommended setting that all unknown sources should be filtered as spam and manually whitelisted by an administrator.

Email whitelist

Under **Email whitelist**, you can review or add whitelisted email sources according to their IP address. Be advised that this is for whitelisting business partners, clients, or internal private email servers:

Enhance pre-delivery message scanning

Keeping **Enhance pre-delivery message scanning** enabled will make Gmail thoroughly analyze and be more suspicious of incoming emails containing suspicious content:

Inbound gateway

In some cases, your business might be using an inbound mail gateway for the prefiltering, archiving, or preprocessing of incoming messages. In this case, you need to set up an inbound mail gateway. To do this, hover your cursor over the **Inbound gateway** section and click **CONFIGURE**, which will appear on the right-hand side, to open the **Add setting | Inbound gateway** form:

First, write a short description for this gateway. This will help as a quick reference in the **General Settings | Inbound gateway** summary:

Then, write the IP address, or range, for this server and choose whether you wish to activate any of the following options:

- **Automatically detect external IP** will make Gmail verify whether an email is emanating from the external IP of a whitelisted server
- **Reject all mail not from gateway IPs** will reject anything that is not coming from your inbound gateway to make sure that nothing is bypassing it
- **Require TLS for connections from email gateways** is a standard that uses **Secure Socket Layer** (**SSL**) encryption technology that helps to prevent attackers from intercepting the message during transportation

We can set up custom spam filtering criteria by enabling the **Message Tagging** option that allows users to define custom spam filters using **regular expressions** (**regex**), either by matching text patterns, complete words, text with variable characters, or even scoring the contents to see how similar they are to a regex and set a threshold based on that score. We will talk more about filtering things by content when we talk about setting up **Objectionable content** in the **Compliance** section.

If we want to rely solely on our inbound gateway's security, we can disable Gmail spam evaluation for content coming from this gateway. In this case, Gmail will only use the header's information for potentially suspicious inbound messages.

Once you are finished setting up the new inbound gateway, click **ADD SETTING** to return to **Settings for Gmail | Advanced Settings**.

Spam

Next, we have the **Spam** section, which allows us to check current approved senders and add new ones. To do so, hover on the section and click **CONFIGURE** on the right to show the **Add setting | Spam** form:

| Spam | Create approved senders lists that bypass the spam folder. | CONFIGURE |
| Not configured yet | | |

As usual, the first thing we need to provide is a short description for this new rule and then we have a few options to define it. The first one offers you the option to **Be more aggressive when filtering spam**, which will lower the threshold score required in terms of considering something suspicious:

Required: enter a short description that will appear within the setting's summary.

All incoming email messages are subjected to Google's spam filters. Messages detected as spam are automatically placed in the spam folder.

Modify this default behavior in the following ways

☑ Be more aggressive when filtering spam.

☑ Bypass spam filters for messages received from internal senders.

Next, we have **Bypass spam filters for messages received from internal senders**, which will disable spam filters for messages sent internally within your business. It's usually best to also check those messages, since many attacks are designed to send messages from a compromised computer within your team to others. If your team uses third-party integration, for example, with Outlook, it's highly advisable to also check internal emails to be able to stop and detect these kinds of attacks early and to take action in relation to the potentially compromised computer.

You can also choose to bypass spam filters from addresses or domains from an approved list. To create a new list, click **Use existing or create a new one**, write a name, and click **CREATE**. You will see the new list added to this section and if you hover over one list, you will see the options to **Edit** its content or **Don't use** it. Select **Edit** to bring up the option to add an email address or a domain to this list. You can also choose to not require sender authentication for these sources:

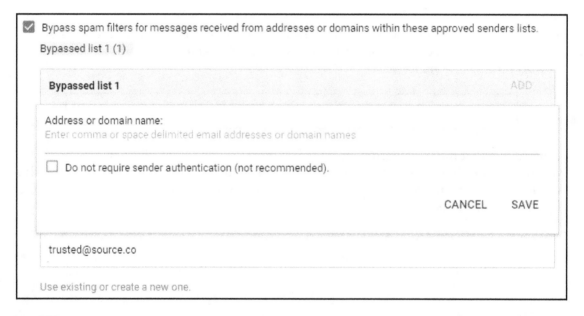

The final option we see allows you to send the spam found using these rules to a specific quarantine list. You can choose the default option, or one of the custom options we created previously:

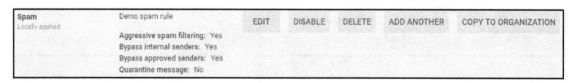

Once you are done, click **ADD SETTING** to save this new spam rule. Once created, you will see it listed in the spam section, along with a basic description, and hovering over it will allow you to **EDIT, DISABLE, DELETE, ADD ANOTHER,** or **COPY TO ORGANIZATION**, which is useful if you are handling more than one domain and you wish to apply the same rule across several domains.

Blocked senders

Finally, we have the **Blocked senders** section, which allows you to define rules that blocks specific emails or domains. Click on **CONFIGURE** and hover over this section to open the **Add setting | Blocked senders** form.

Adding **Blocked senders** is very straightforward. Similar to the previous settings, we start by providing a short description for this rule, which will be used for quick reference at **General Settings | Blocked senders**:

Blocked senders Not configured yet	Block or approve specific senders based on email address or domain. CONFIGURE

In the first field, you can **Add addresses or domains that you want to automatically reject messages from**. You can opt for **Use existing or create a new one**:

1. Add addresses or domains that you want to automatically reject messages from

  No lists used yet. Use existing or create a new one.

The second field allows you to add a custom **rejection notice** that will override whatever default you have when something is rejected due to this rule:

2. Edit the default rejection notice Optional

  Enter customized rejection notice. (e.g. "Your email has been rejected because it violates organization policy").

Finally, you can add exceptions to this rule by selecting lists of domains of addresses that should bypass this rule, even if they match one of the lists added in the first step:

Once you click **Add setting**, the form will close and you will see your new rule, along with any previous rule you may have, each of which will show the description you provided, the number of blocked lists, and whether there are bypass rules enabled:

> **Blocked senders**
> Locally applied
>
> **Blocked senders**
> Locally applied

> Unwanted senders example
>
> Blocked senders message sets: 1
> Bypass approved senders: Yes
>
> Another unwanted senders example
>
> Blocked senders message sets: 2
> Bypass approved senders: No

If you wish to add a new rule, hover over any of the elements and click **ADD ANOTHER**.

Compliance

Compliance is a very powerful tool that allows you to set up rules to control inbound, outbound, and internal messages based on their content and define whether they should be rejected, quarantined, or delivered with some modifications.

Email and chat auto-deletion

First, we have the setup for **Email and chat auto-deletion** policies. By default, **Do not delete email and chat messages automatically** is selected, but you can change it so that messages are automatically deleted after a certain period—which, by default, is 30 days.

Once the selected period has passed, you can either choose to **Move messages to the Trash folder** or **Delete messages permanently**:

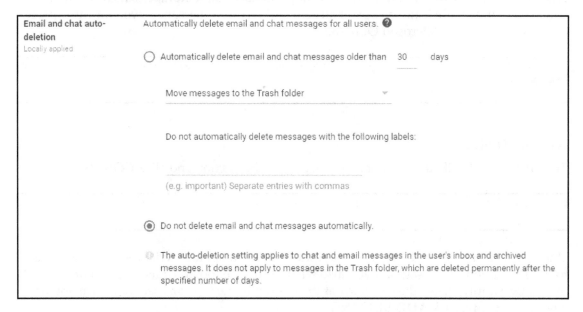

Keep in mind that messages in the trash folder will be permanently deleted after a few days, so it's a good idea to move them there first instead of immediately deleting them to minimize the potential of unwanted deletions and data loss.

Optical Character Recognition

The second option allows you to enable **Optical Character Recognition (OCR),** which is a machine learning-powered feature that allows Gmail to read text in JPG, PNG, GIF, or TIFF images for content compliance rule violations in attachments. Be aware that this will not work on images inside PDFs or Microsoft Word files, and that it's not 100% accurate, but still adds a nice layer of security:

Optical Character Recognition (OCR) Locally applied	☑ Enable OCR for email attachments.
	⊕ Optical Character Recognition (OCR) setting applies only to licensed users with the appropriate G Suite offering.

Comprehensive mail storage

Next, you will have the option to enable **Comprehensive mail storage**, which will make Gmail store in **Google Vault** a copy of all sent and received messages, even for third-party email servers such as Microsoft Outlook:

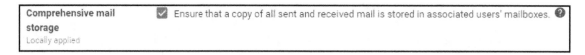

Append footer

To add a footer to all outbound emails, hover over this section and click **CONFIGURE**:

Once the form appears, add a short description of this footer and write the footer you wish to use for outbound messages. If you also wish to add the footer for messages sent internally, simply enable the checkbox at the bottom in the **Options** section. Once you have everything ready, click **ADD SETTING**.

In the **Append footer** form, start by writing a short description for this footer and then write the footer as you wish in the text box:

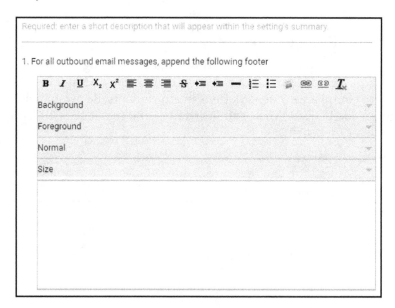

Optionally, you can choose to also append this footer to messages sent within the team:

Restrict delivery

In some cases, you may need to restrict all inbound and outbound messages to pre-approved lists. To do this, hover over **Restrict delivery** and click **CONFIGURE**:

In the form, start by providing the usual short description, and then select or create approved lists for inbound and outbound messages. In the second field, you can write a custom message that will be sent to senders of all rejected messages:

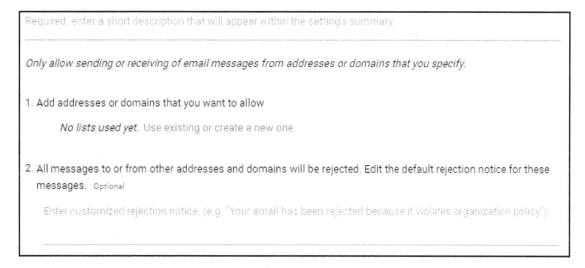

Finally, you can select **Bypass this setting for internal messages**, which is enabled by default. Once you are done, click **ADD SETTING**:

Content compliance

To set up advanced content filters that will search for specific words, phrases, or even patterns, hover over the **Content Compliance** section and click **CONFIGURE**:

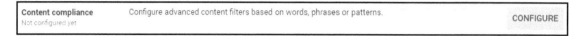

Start by adding a short description to your new compliance rule and then select which messages should be affected by it—you can choose from inbound, outbound, and internal sending or receiving.

In the second part, you will have the option to add the expressions you wish to detect and choose whether the rule will apply when any of these has a match, or only when the message has all of them. Click **ADD** to add a new expression rule and select the type of expression you wish to use by clicking on **Simple content match** to see the different options:

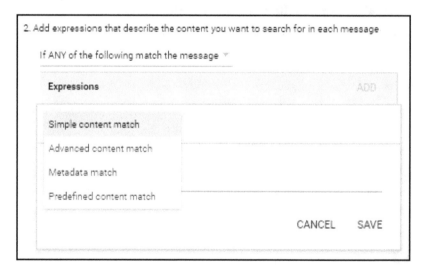

- **Simple content match** allows you to write a word or phrase to look for.
- **Advanced content match** is similar, but you can choose which part of the message to search and the matching criteria before adding the word or phrase you wish to look for.
- **Metadata match** offers quick filters based on metadata attributes in the messages. You can choose to use **Message authentication**, **Source IP range**, **Secure Transport Layer**, **Message Size**, and **Gmail confidential mode**.

- **Predefined content match** is extremely useful because it provides you with several predefined advanced content match rules. They can be in a global context, such as **Credit card number**, or country-specific, such as **United States SSN** or **Mexico CURP**.

In the third part of the form, you can select what to do **If the above expressions match**, giving you the option to **Modify message**, **Reject Message**, or **Quarantine message**. Ideally, you want to choose **Quarantine message** and move the messages to a named quarantine so that the administrator can review the incoming messages and choose the appropriate action, and even create a new exception if needed.

At the bottom of this panel, you will see a **Show options** string. Clicking it will show a few additional setups:

- **Address lists** allows you to bypass or apply these rules to just a specific list.
- **Account types to affect** sets the kind of accounts that will be affected by this rule.
- **Envelope filter** allows you to apply the rule for inbound and outbound messages to a specific email, addresses that match a regex, or specific groups in this domain, as can be seen in the following screenshot:

```
A. Address lists
    ☐  Use address lists to bypass or control application of this setting
        ○  Bypass this setting for specific addresses / domains
        ○  Only apply this setting for specific addresses / domains

B. Account types to affect
        ☑  Users
        ☐  Groups
        ☐  Unrecognized / Catch-all

C. Envelope filter
        ☐  Only affect specific envelope senders
        ☐  Only affect specific envelope recipients
```

Once you are finished setting up your rules, click **ADD SETTING** to add the new rule.

Objectionable content

The next general setting is **Objectionable content**, where you can configure filters using lists of suspicious words, such as `confidential`, `prototype`, and `secret`. To create a new rule, hover over this section and click **CONFIGURE**:

1. The first step is to write the usual short description for this new rule and then select whether you wish to target **Inbound**, **Outbound**, **Internal - sending** or **Internal - receiving** messages:

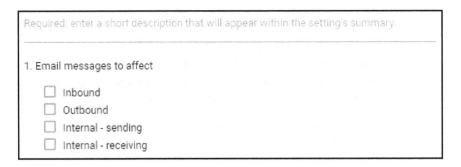

2. In the second field, click **ADD** to write a word or words you wish to target. You can separate them simply by using spaces, and after you click **SAVE**; they will be stored separately. If you hover over any word on the list, you will see the options to **Edit** or **Delete** that word:

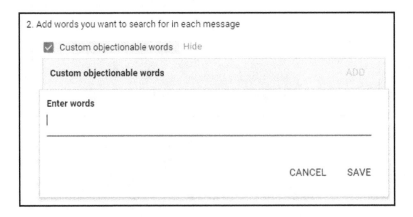

3. In the third field, you can define what should happen when this rule is applied:
    - The first option will allow you to **Modify message** and select the changes you wish to apply:

```
┌─────────────────────────────────────────────┐
│  Modify message          ▼                   │
│  ─────────────────────────────               │
│                                              │
│  Headers                                     │
│  ☐ Add X-Gm-Original-To header               │
│  ☐ Add X-Gm-Spam and X-Gm-Phishy headers     │
│  ☐ Add custom headers                        │
│                                              │
│  Subject                                     │
│  ☐ Prepend custom subject                    │
│                                              │
│  Route                                       │
│  ☐ Change route                              │
│                                              │
│  Envelope recipient                          │
│  ☐ Change envelope recipient                 │
│                                              │
│  Spam                                        │
│  ☐ Bypass spam filter for this message       │
│                                              │
│  Attachments                                 │
│  ☐ Remove attachments from message           │
│                                              │
│  Also deliver to                             │
│  ☐ Add more recipients                       │
│                                              │
│  Encryption (onward delivery only)           │
│  ☐ Require secure transport (TLS)            │
└─────────────────────────────────────────────┘
```

- **Headers**: Change the headers.
- **Subject**: Prepend a custom subject
- **Route**: Change the route
- **Envelope recipient**: Change the envelope recipient
- **Spam**: Bypass spam filters
- **Attachments**: Remove attachments
- **Also deliver to**: Send a copy to an address such as a security compliance group
- **Encryption (onward delivery only)**: Require the use of secure transport layer encryption.

4. You can also choose to route the message directly to one of the quarantines:

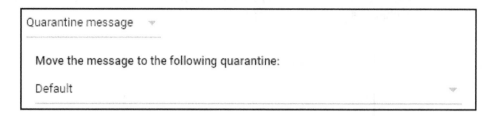

5. Alternatively, you can just reject the message and optionally send a custom rejection notice for this rule:

Attachment compliance

Attachments are particularly prone to leaks and attacks and, with Gmail for Business, you can create rules to control them based on their type, name, and size so that you can define how they should be handled.

Gmail uses binary file-type detection for most common types to prevent users from trying to bypass the rules by changing the file extension. To get started, click on **CONFIGURE** to set up a new rule:

Attachment compliance Not configured yet	Configure attachment filters based on file type, file name and message size.	CONFIGURE

Let's start by adding a short description for this rule and then selecting the type of messages this rule should target:

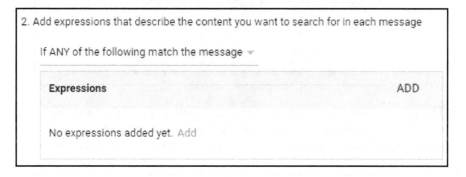

The next step is to define what this rule will be targeting in the messages. You can create expressions that target attachments by type, name, or size. You must choose whether you need to make this rule active if any of the conditions are a match, or only when all the conditions are met, choose the one that you need, and click **ADD** to add a new expression. You can add many different expressions, even if they are of different types. This gives you great flexibility so you can be as broad or accurate as required:

- The first option is to match them by **File Type**. You will see a list of the supported file types, so just select the ones you wish to target. You can also define **Custom file types**. If you wish to add many file types, write them, separated by commas. By the way, there is no need to worry about executable files since they are rejected by default:

File type   ▾

The attachment is of type

Office documents (.doc, .xls, .ppt...)
    ☐ Office documents which are encrypted
    ☐ Office documents which are not encrypted
☐ Video and multimedia (.mpg, .mov, .avi...)
☐ Music and sound (.mp3, .wav, .aiff...)
☐ Images (.jpg, .gif, .png...)
Compressed files and archives (.zip, .tar, .gz...)
    ☐ Compressed files and archives which are encrypted
    ☐ Compressed files and archives which are not encrypted

Custom file types - Match files based on file name extension

    e.g. zip, rar

    ☐ Also match files based on file format (supported types)

Note: For your protection, all executables are automatically rejected.

- The next option allows you to target attachments by **File name** by simply writing what you want to target as part of the filename. It's best to keep this as short as possible, but you can target numerous filename expressions if you so require:

File name   ▾

The attachment file name contains

- The last option is to target attachments according to their **Message size**. This will include both the body and all attachments and it will target all messages above the number of megabytes you write in the field, which must be a round number:

The last setting of an attachment compliance rule defines what must be done with messages that meets the rule's criteria, thereby allowing you to do any of the following:

- **Modify message**: Let it through, but with modifications, such as removing the attachment
- **Reject message**: Reject the entire message and send a notification back to the sender
- **Quarantine message**: Route the message to one of the quarantines so an administrator can choose what to do

Secure transport (TLS) compliance

The **Transport Layer Security** (**TLS**) protocol provides safe and private communication by generating a unique key for symmetric encryption so that the information cannot be read or modified by third parties. It also allows you to authenticate one or both servers using public-key cryptography (certificates). To set this up, hover over the section and click **CONFIGURE**:

Secure transport (TLS) compliance	Require TLS when communicating with specified domains.	CONFIGURE
Not configured yet		

Start by writing the usual short description for this setup and, in the first field, select whether you want to target inbound or outbound messages. You can also choose to only use it for outbound messages when required by another setting:

> Required: enter a short description that will appear within the setting's summary.
>
> 1. Email messages to affect
>
> ☐ Inbound - all messages
> ☐ Outbound - all messages
>   ☐ Outbound - messages requiring Secure Transport via another setting

In the second field, you can select or create the address lists where Gmail will be using TLS:

> 2. Use TLS for secure transport when corresponding with these domains / email addresses.
>
> *No lists used yet.* Use existing or create a new one.

If you enable the last option, Gmail will require the receiving server to provide a valid certificate signed by a certificate authority. This is done to prevent fake third-party servers from pretending to be one of your team's contacts:

> 3. Options
>
> ☐ Require CA signed cert when delivering outbound to the above-specified TLS-enabled domains.

Routing

Gmail allows you to set up advanced email routing and delivery options so teams' communication can flow as needed. This section provides general routing options that will be applied in addition to any specific routing scenario defined in other security settings.

Outbound gateway

Here, you can route all the outbound messages to an **outbound mail gateway server,** also known as **smart host.**

Outbound mail gateway servers are used by some organizations to process messages before being forwarded to their recipient, for archiving in a similar way to Google Vault, and for detecting spam using a private service:

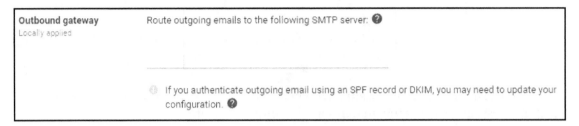

Routing

Many rules may define specific routing rules as part of them, but here you define routing rules in a more generic way by targeting specific email addresses, mails sent to one of the organization's groups, or use a regular expression to search for name patterns.

To add a new setting, hover over the section and click **CONFIGURE**:

Start by giving this rule a short description and, in the first section, select the inbound and outbound targeting that will be applied:

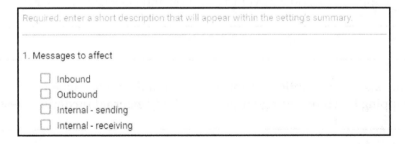

The second section allows you to specify whether you wish to apply the rule you are creating just to a specific envelope, **senders** or **recipients**. If you don't select anything, the rule will be applied to both:

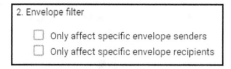

And, in the last section, we will define whether you wish to perform some modifications, send the message to one of the quarantines, or simply reject it:

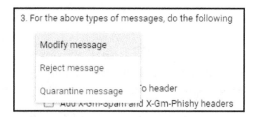

Recipient address map

Gmail allows you to map up to twelve recipient aliases to a single email address in what is known as a virtual user table that can store up to 2,000 entries. This allows you to distribute inbound email through your team in a very efficient way.

To add a new mapping rule, hover over this section and click **CONFIGURE**:

Start by writing a short description for this routing and then select whether you wish to apply this mapping to **All incoming messages** or **Only external incoming messages**:

In the second part of the form, you define whether the message should also be sent to the original destination. If disabled, the message will only be received by addresses we are going to map on the next part:

In the third option, you can add individually the mappings you wish to apply by adding a list of addresses, separated by commas.

First, write the destination address you need to map and then the address you want to map it to. For example, if you wish to map the same address to different destinations, you will have to add three lines, all starting with the same original address, but with a different destination in the second field:

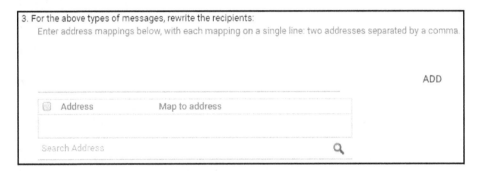

The final option will add a copy of the original intended destination in the header:

```
4. Options
    ☐ Add X-Gm-Original-To header
```

Inbound email journal acceptance in Vault

Vault allows your domain to perform message journaling from Microsoft Exchange Journaling so that administrators can perform eDiscovery and find specific content with ease.

In this section, you can overlook the current mapping rules, edit them, or add new ones. To get started, hover over the section and click on **CONFIGURE**:

Inbound email journal acceptance in Vault Not configured yet	Specify a receiving email address and access controls for accepting journal messages.	CONFIGURE

1. Now, write a short description that will help you quickly identify this rule later and write the address that your organization will use to receive the journal messages:

   > Required: enter a short description that will appear within the setting's summary.
   >
   > 1. Receive journal messages at the following address

2. You can also limit the acceptance of journal messages to specific senders in order to avoid unwanted content filtering in the organization's Vault:

   > 2. Only accept journal messages from this sender   Optional

3. Under the third option, specify an address that will receive a notification when a journal message has bounced:

   > 3. Bounce email address for failed journal deliveries

4. Enabling the fourth option will **Reject journal messages that are not DKIM/SPF authenticated**:

   > 4. ☑ Reject journal messages that are not DKIM/SPF authenticated

5. To **Reject journal messages for unrecognized recipients**, enable the fifth option:

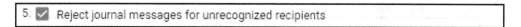

6. The sixth option allows you to limit the acceptance of journal messages to specific IP addresses or ranges:

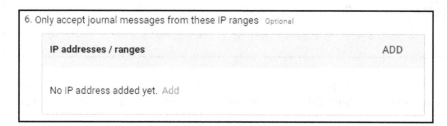

7. The final option allows you to define a specific rejection notice that will be sent to all the messages that are bounced because of this rule:

Non-Gmail mailbox

This will allow you to route all messages to an external non-Google SMTP server and mailbox, as well as effectively disable the Gmail mailbox, and all users will depend on the external mailbox, such as Microsoft Exchange. You may configure more than one external mailbox.

To set up your external mailbox, hover over this section and click **CONFIGURE**:

Non-Gmail mailbox	Reroute messages to a non-Google SMTP server. Optionally, schedule periodic delivery of summary messages, which list recently quarantined spam.	CONFIGURE
Not configured yet		

Start by giving this a short description that will be used for quick reference on the settings summary and choosing a mail server:

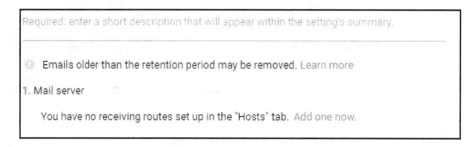

If you have no server configurations saved, just click on **Add one now**. In the form, start by writing the name of the new SMTP server and add the port and IP if it is a **Single host:**

You can also use **Multiple hosts** using the **Primary** and **Secondary** hosts lists. Also, you can define how much load you wish to route to each of these hosts:

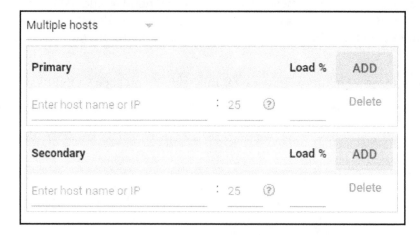

Click **SAVE** once you are finished defining the new route and it will be automatically applied to your mailbox routing rule.

The second section will give you the option to **Allow users to login to Message Center** so they can access the messages flagged as spam by the Gmail server. It can also be used to see the messages routed to the external mailboxes:

In the third section, you can **Enable periodic summaries** of the quarantined messages to be sent to this mailbox. Also, you can define when the summaries should be sent:

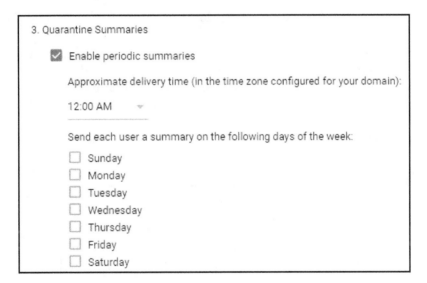

Enabling the option in the final section will allow users to report spam using the external mailbox to the Gmail servers:

4. Options

    ☐ Allow users to report spam (recommended)

SMTP relay service

We have talked about how to reroute all your organization's inbound messages to an external server, and now we will learn how to route the outbound messages through Google so that your organization can use the advanced filtering and routing options.

To set up the **SMTP relay service**, hover over this section and click **CONFIGURE** to add a new rule. Similar to other sections, you may add a variety of rules to accommodate complex routing requirements:

The first section lets you define the senders allowed through this SMTP relay rule:

- **Only registered Apps users in my domains** will only allow users who are registered to messages.
- **Only addresses in my domains** will allow unregistered users to relay messages as long as they have an address from one of the account domains. Use this to create rules that allow messages to be relayed from third-party applications. I would recommend that you create a relay rule for every third-party application you wish to authorize.
- **Any addresses** will allow any relay request to use this service. Avoid using this option:

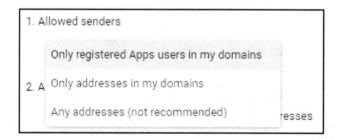

In the second section, you can define whether you wish to use the authentication requirements for the relayed messages. The first option allows you to **Only accept mail from the specified IP addresses**.

After enabling this option, click on **ADD IP RANGE** and start by writing a short description for this server and then write the IP address or range you wish to whitelist. IPv6 addresses are supported too.

Click **SAVE** to finish adding this address, and feel free to add more if you need by clicking **ADD ANOTHER**. You can also **EDIT, DISABLE,** or **DELETE** already stored addresses by hovering over their description and clicking on the option you need:

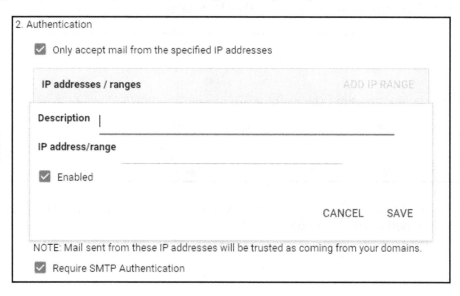

Finally, select whether TLS encryption is expected from this source to prevent potentially fake messages from being relayed by Gmail:

Remember to click **SAVE** to apply this new configuration.

Alternate secure route

You can set an **Alternate secure route** to use a third-party encryption service of your choice for messages that require TLS. To set this up, hover over the section and click **CONFIGURE** to add the details of the encryption service. Bear in mind that you can only set one route for this purpose:

Alternate secure route Not configured yet	Use alternate secure route when secure transport (TLS) is required.	CONFIGURE

Start by setting a short description for the encryption service, enable the **Use alternate secure route when secure transport (TLS) is required** option, and then select the mailing route or choose to add a new one. We will talk more about how to add email routes in the following sections, where we will explore the **Hosts** tab:

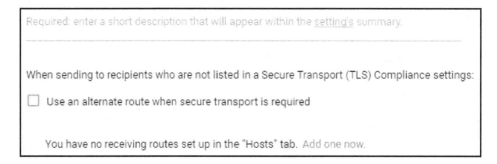

You can now define more detailed inbound, outbound and internal routing policies. In the next section we will learn how to define

Hosts

Typically, Gmail uses direct mail delivery. However, **Hosts** allows you to define advanced mail delivery routes that will allow you to route mails to third-party servers, such as Microsoft Exchange. In this section, you can add new routes and edit or delete existing ones:

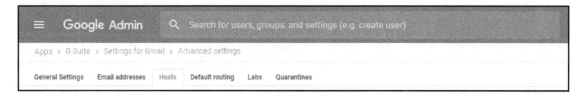

Add mail route

You should add a mail route for each external server you need. To do so, click on **ADD ROUTE** in the top-right section to bring up the form and start by writing a short description and enable to **Use an alternate route when secure transport is required**.

In the first part, you have two options. The first option allows you to set a **Single host** by writing the host name or IP and the port you wish to connect; usually, the port is 25:

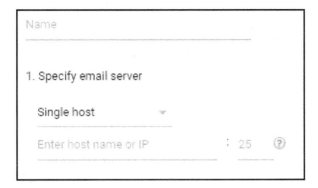

You can also set up a list of multiple primary and secondary hosts, write the host or IP in the type you wish to add, and the port and the load percentage you wish to route to that server. You can add many hosts to each list if necessary:

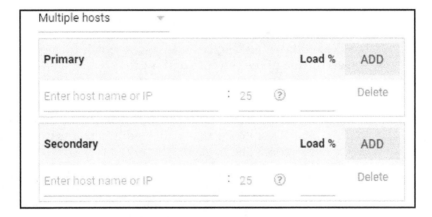

Finally, you can choose to enforce some advanced security features for this route. The first option will make Gmail **Perform MX lookup on host**, and require TLS encryption with or without a certificate validated by a CA:

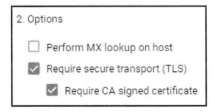

Once you are ready, click **SAVE** to add the new mailing route.

Sending emails to groups

Groups are mailing lists that facilitate communication within your business. You can set groups to talk about specific subjects, such as team objectives or results, form teams, or even handle inbound emails from clients since every group has its own dedicated email address so that people can write to that address and be sure the message will be routed to the right people.

When a message arrives at a group address, it will be forwarded to all its members who will see it in their inbox as a message coming from that group.

To create a new group, go to the administrator's home page:

1. Click **Groups**
2. Click **Create a Group**
3. Choose:
    - A **Name for the group**.
    - A **Group email address**.
    - A **Description** of the purpose of this group.
    - An **Access level**:
        - **Public**: Use this option to allow the entire team to subscribe, view members, and post and read content. Despite the name, this group remains private within the domain.
        - **Team**: With this option, only managers can subscribe members to this group, but anyone can view members, and post and read content. With this access level, you can also select whether you wish to allow anyone to post to this message group by writing an email to the address; even people outside your team.
        - **Announcement-only**: This will restrict posting to, and viewing of, the members' list to administrators. The entire team can subscribe and read content.
        - **Restricted**: With this level, only managers can subscribe members and only members can post and read content.
    - The last option will enable all members of your team to be added automatically to this group.
4. Click **Create**.

That's it! Now your team can start using this group and you can also add it to your routing and security rules.

 You can easily create a customer support address by creating a Group called Support, giving it an access level of Team, and selecting **Also allow anyone on the internet to post messages** . Then, you can add all the people within the company that will help with customer support to this group. For example, all emails written to support@cesarstechinsights.net will be received by all the members of the Support group.

Summary

Congratulations! Now you know the capabilities, security features, and protocols of Gmail for Business, allowing you to perform the necessary configurations for a new or existing domain.

Unwanted emails waste time and can lead to all kinds of security problems. In this chapter, you have learned how to configure spam detection, routing, and analysis. We also learned how to set trusted emails and domains, and how to enforce validations using security protocols and certificates.

You also learned how to allow users to delegate access to others in a safe way and how to create groups so users can subscribe or send messages to colleagues who are interested in a specific task or topic.

A number of corporations own private servers or are migrating from Microsoft Outlook, so now you know how to integrate different mailing services with Microsoft Outlook or other third-party services, or even fully bypass Gmail and route everything to private instances. With this knowledge, you should be ready to handle even complex requirements.

Email is just one of the many ways G Suite for Business facilitates communication and coordination. In the next chapter, we will learn about team collaboration with G Suite, where we will explore how to make best use of the platform to take the team's collaboration and communication to the next level.

Team Collaboration with G Suite 3

G Suite is designed to address your team's collaboration and communication needs. In this chapter, you will learn how to use Calendar to its fullest potential, allowing teams to share calendars, send reminders, find the best time for a meeting, and reserve the ideal place for it.

Real-time communication is also essential for a modern team. To that end, Hangouts allows you to host chats and video conferences with up to 25 members, while Google Drive allows teams to share files with up to 200 people and host up to 50 of them to collaborate in real time on a single document, spreadsheet, or presentation.

Social media is very popular these days, so we will learn how to set up a private social media platform for our domain using G+ so your team can use it to grow ideas and projects internally, or engage with customers externally.

Sometimes your team needs an intuitive email address, such as `support@`, `sales@`, or `contact@`, and to be able to trust that that message will be seen by the right people. In this chapter, you will learn the settings you need for groups to facilitate the routing of messages to groups of users.

Sharing information is a basic need in a team, but doing it safely is hard without the right technology. In this chapter, you will learn how to set up Google Drive so that your team can share files or collaborate on documents in real time using Google Docs, a full office suite in the cloud, meaning you don't need to install additional software to use it or worry about data being stored on devices.

Let's walk through the administration setup, so that you'll be able to do the following:

- Configure Calendar for Business
- Configure Google Groups
- Create and administer private G+ communities and collections
- Enable real-time communication and collaboration with Hangouts
- Search, share, and collaborate with Google Drive

Coordinating your team with Calendar for Business

Calendar is usually the main tool to coordinate activities within a team, allowing members to see each other's available time slots and also find which rooms with the right capacity and features will be available at that time. Calendar will update everyone's calendar in real time and send reminders, and has other useful features that facilitate effective resource management.

The **Room Insights Dashboard** allows managers to analyze how resources are being used and fine-tune them to maximize the team's evolving needs by monitoring which are the most and least used rooms and features, and to make adjustments accordingly.

Let's explore how to set up the Calendar configurations. To find the Calendar settings, take these steps from the administrator home page:

1. Select **Apps**
2. Click on **G Suite**
3. Select **Calendar**

Sharing settings

Being able to share calendar events with colleagues with ease is vital for effective team collaboration. With team policies, you can determine how much information can be shared internally and externally.

External sharing options for primary calendars

Here, we define the policies for sharing calendar information outside the organization. Select the option that best suits the team's needs:

External sharing options for primary calendars Locally applied	Outside Cesar Anton Dorantes - set user ability for primary calendars By default, primary calendars are not shared outside Cesar Anton Dorantes. Select the highest level of sharing that you want to allow for your users. ◉ Only free/busy information (hide event details) ○ Share all information, but outsiders cannot change calendars ○ Share all information, and outsiders can change calendars ○ Share all information, and allow managing of calendars

- **Only free/busy information (hide event details)**: People will only be able to see if the person is busy or available
- **Share all information, but outsiders cannot change calendars**: All calendar information will be available but only for reading
- **Share all information, and outsiders can change calendars**: All calendar information will be available and anyone can make changes
- **Share all information, and allow managing of calendars**: Allows users to see all information, make changes, and manage sharing

Now that we have the external sharing options covered, let's learn how to configure **Internal sharing options**.

Internal sharing options for primary calendars

Internal calendar sharing defines whether a user allows others in the organization to see their calendar information. As an admin, you can choose the default setting for all users. Users can later change their Calendar settings manually:

Internal sharing options for primary calendars Locally applied	**Within Cesar Anton Dorantes - set default** Users will be able to change this default setting. Super Admins have 'Make changes and manage sharing' access to all calendars on the domain. ❷
	○ No sharing
	○ Only free/busy information (hide event details)
	◉ Share all information

- **No sharing**: Internal calendar sharing is disabled
- **Only free/busy information (hide event details)**: Other members of the organization can only see if the person is busy
- **Share all information**: Other members of the organization can see all calendar details

Sharing calendars is very useful for coordinating events and even conversations. In the next section, we will configure **Video Call**s for Calendar events.

Video Calls

Calendar events can have a unique Hangout video call associated with them. Even if a meeting will be in person, it's usually a good idea to facilitate joining remotely, in case someone is running late or can't make it for any reason:

Video Calls Locally applied	☑ Automatically add video calls to events created by a user

Enable this setting so that all calendar events get a Hangout URL by default. Repeated events use the same address across all event series, making it easy to bookmark links.

External Invitations

It's common to send invitations to lists of people, but sometimes, this can lead to accidentally inviting external users. You can choose to give users a warning every time they send a Calendar invitation to users that are not part of a particular domain:

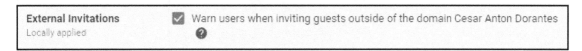

Sharing calendars will facilitate coordination in the organization. In the next section, we will learn how to use **Resources** to provide physical locations for events within an organization.

Resource management

Users can point to a building resource as the location for a Calendar event, which, for the attendees, provides a reference on how to get to the meeting. For the organizer, it facilitates finding the right resource for the event depending on the location, capacity, features, and availability.

Let's explore how to register buildings and the resources available in them:

> **Resources**
>
> Define resources that are available for users to schedule on their calendars, such as meeting rooms, projectors, company cars, or other shared equipment.

Buildings

Every resource must be associated with a building, so you must first define all the buildings in your organization. You can define buildings one by one using the web platform, or create a CSV file with all the building details and upload it to define all buildings in a single operation:

To administer buildings, go to the upper-left side of the **Resource management** section, click on the arrow, ▼, and select **Buildings** from the options. This will show you a list of all registered buildings so that you can edit or delete them. You can also add new ones or download a CSV file with all the buildings' information. This file is very useful as a backup, and can be used to migrate this configuration to other accounts:

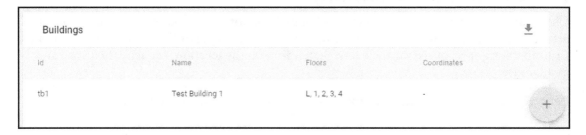

Adding new buildings

To register a new building, click on the yellow ⊕ icon and fill in the form with at least the **Id**, **Name**, and **Floors** information, and click **ADD BUILDING** when you finish, to save it:

Bulk uploading building settings

Instead of manually defining or updating new buildings, it's usually faster to upload a CSV file with the entire buildings configuration. The easiest way to do this is to use a CSV backup file like the one that we previously downloaded.

To bulk upload buildings, hover over the yellow 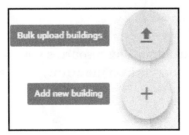 icon and click on the **Bulk upload buildings** icon:

CSV files are pretty simple text files that describe a table using line breaks to separate rows, and commas to separate columns. The first row contains the headers and it is expected that the following rows will have the same columns as the headers. To build descriptions, your headers must be `Building Id,Building Name,Floors,Description,Coordinates`. Each of the following rows defines a building.

This is how a CSV file with a single building would look:

```
Building Id,Building Name,Floors,Description,Coordinates
tb1,Test Building 1,"L,1,2,3,4",First test building,
```

Once you have your CSV file ready, click **ATTACH CSV**, select the file, and finally, click **UPLOAD**:

Add new buildings and edit existing buildings by uploading a csv file of buildings and their info. After the import a confirmation and details about upload errors will be sent to

contact@cesarstechinsights.net.

ATTACH CSV

Not sure how to get started?

Learn how to prepare your building data in our help center article.

Download blank CSV template

Download your buildings in a CSV file

Resources

Just like we did for buildings, to administer resources you must go the upper-left side of the **Resource management** section, click on the arrow, ▼ , and select **Resources** from the options:

This section will show you the buildings on the left and then all the resources (or the ones associated with a specific building) on the right. In this section, you can also add a new resource, download a CSV backup with the resources, manage resource features, or add filters to facilitate finding resources in the list:

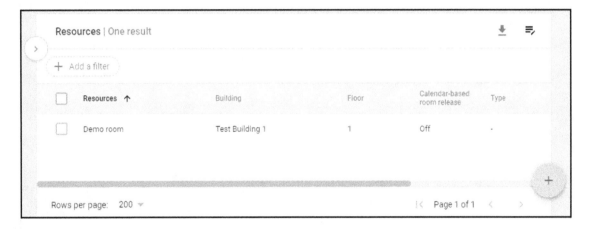

To make best use of Calendar, it's important to take the time to define and maintain the **Resources** registry so that users can easily choose one when creating a new Calendar meeting.

Adding new resources

To register a new resource, click on the yellow ⊕ icon and fill in the form, describing the new resource and to which building it belongs. It's strongly advised to fill this in as much as possible, and to keep it updated so that users can use this information when choosing a location for an event.

In **Room settings** you can **Allow calendar-based room release**, which will automatically release booked rooms that are no longer needed because it was cancelled or the attendants declined the invitation:

Click **ADD RESOURCE** to save the new resource.

Managing resource features

Resources may have features such as a phone or a webcam in them, so it's useful to have them available in the system so that users can take that into account when choosing a location.

To manage resource features, click on the 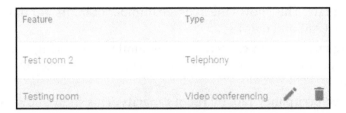 icon that is next to the download all ↓ icon at the top-right part of the platform. Calendar allows you to add up to 100 features in a domain. This is for the total sum of all features in all resources:

Feature	Type
Test room 2	Telephony
Testing room	Video conferencing

Defining features is pretty straightforward; you write the name or a short description of the feature and select its type:

Now that you have defined some resources, it's time to learn how the **Room Insights Dashboard** can help you monitor resources.

Exploring the Room Insights Dashboard

Another key feature of Calendar's resource management are usage reports:

Analyzing reports allows you to make informed decisions when looking for ways to add or optimize resources.

Room usage

This part of the report allows administrators to analyze room usage within a specific time frame by showing the following charts:

- **Booking rate**: This shows the average number of hours per day that were booked between 8 AM and 6 PM.
- **Booking rate by room capacity**: This is similar to **Booking rate**, but the average is based on room capacity instead. This helps you to notice the most in-demand capacity.
- **Estimated occupancy rate by room capacity**: This shows how full rooms of different capacities were.
- **Booking rate by time of day**: This shows the percentage of rooms that are occupied at different times of the day.
- **Booking distribution**: This groups rooms by average booked hours per day.
- **Most used rooms**: This shows the most id-demand resources with their booking and occupancy rates.
- **Least used rooms**: This shows the resources in least demand with their booking and occupancy rates.

Room release

If **Room release** is enabled, this section will allow administrators to analyze how much time was effectively used after a room was automatically released.

Room release uses the following charts:

- **Released time**: This shows the total amount of time that was released
- **Rebooked time**: This shows how much of the released time was actually rebooked
- **Unreleased time**: This is the amount of hours that were not released, but might have been with different settings

A resource that is usually rebooked shortly after being released is usually an indicator that you should analyze what is causing users to look for it, and plan how to add alternative resources.

General settings

The **General settings** section allows you to define the external sharing options of secondary calendars. These are calendars that are specific to a single user and each user can set different calendars to separate events in custom categories, as well as being able to share just one kind of event, instead of the full calendar.

External sharing options for secondary calendars

Let's define the setting options for when users share calendars with people outside their organization, as follows:

External sharing options for secondary calendars	Outside Cesar Anton Dorantes - set user ability for secondary calendars
	By default, secondary calendars are not shared outside Cesar Anton Dorantes. Select the highest level of sharing that you want to allow for your users.
	○ Only free/busy information (hide event details)
	● Share all information, but outsiders cannot change calendars
	○ Share all information, and outsiders can change calendars
	○ Share all information, and allow managing of calendars

- **Only free/busy information (hide event details)**: Selecting this will only share whether the person is available or not in a time frame
- **Share all information, but outsiders cannot change calendars**: This will allow external users to see all secondary calendar event details, including the guests list but not private addresses
- **Share all information, and outsiders can change calendars**: This will allow external users to see and update secondary calendar events, including the guests list and their addresses
- **Share all information, and allow managing of calendars**: This will allow external users to manage secondary calendar events

Internal sharing options for secondary calendars

Now it's time to define the default limitations of sharing secondary calendars internally. Users can change these settings manually for their own calendar:

Internal sharing options for secondary calendars	Within Cesar Anton Dorantes - set default Users will be able to change this default setting. Super Admins have 'Make changes and manage sharing' access to all calendars on the domain. ❷ ◯ No sharing ◯ Only free/busy information (hide event details) ◉ Share all information

- **No sharing**: Sharing calendars internally is disabled by default
- **Only free/busy information (hide event details)**: By default, users can only share events if they are available or not in a given time frame
- **Share all information**: This makes all calendar information accessible inside the organization

The Manage User Data section

The **Manage User Data** section is used to cancel or transfer all of the events in one user's calendar to another member of the organization:

- **Event cancellation/transfer**: Transfers are done by simply providing both of the users' addresses:

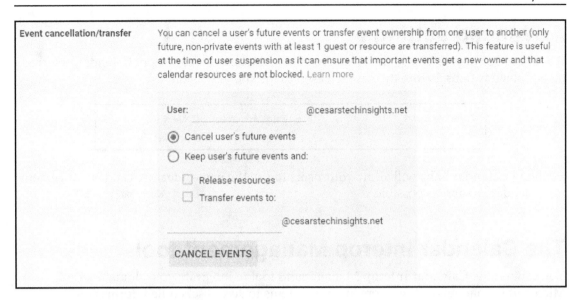

- **Events of deleted users**: You can enable the **Events of deleted users** option if you wish to automatically cancel all events for deleted user accounts. When a member leaves the organization, as an administrator, you need to think about how to handle the information left behind in the system. This option will automatically cancel all events the user created:

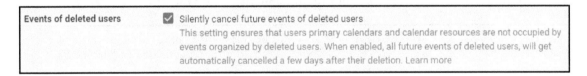

At this point, we have covered the basic **Settings for Calendar**. In the next section, you will learn what you can do with **Advanced settings**.

Advanced settings

Advanced settings offer you the option to enable the newest features of Calendar, referred to as **Calendar Labs**, before they are released to the stable version:

Enabling **Calendar Labs** will allow your users to use the newest features and enhancements for Calendar as soon as possible.

The Calendar Interop Management tool

You can use the **Calendar Interop Management** tool to integrate your domain with Microsoft Exchange to allow users in both systems to access schedule information.

Exchange Web Services settings

In this section, you should provide the **Exchange Web Services** (**EWS**) server associated with your Exchange server, and the **Exchange Role account** and its associated password. This account must be reserved only for moving data between systems:

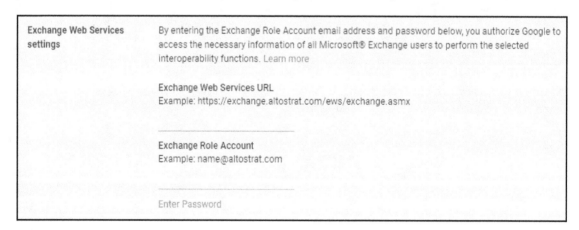

Now that we have a role account, we can proceed and define **Interoperability features**.

Interoperability features

Interoperability features allow you to define the level of detail that will be shared between platforms about users' events. Use these to limit the calendar information that will be available on third-party systems:

- **No information visible**: This setting will block information.
- **Free/busy information visible**: This option will only share whether the user is available in a given time frame.
- **Event details visible**: Event details will be shared between systems. Use this to get a deeper level of integration.

Setting up Google Groups

Google Groups for Business allows your team to create discussion groups for your team to follow up and discuss specific topics, allowing you to route messages of a specific topic to all of the interested members of your organization.

When a group is created, an email address is created for it (such as `group@yourdomain.com`). This allows users to send messages to an address related to a topic or project (such as `support@yourdomain.com` or `coolproject@yourdomain.com`) and it will be forwarded to the other members. This approach is also safer, since the sender doesn't need to know who the members of this group are.

To find **Groups** settings, take these steps from the administrator home page:

1. Select **Apps**
2. Click on **G Suite**
3. Select **Groups for Business**

To choose the right **Sharing settings**, you should consider how the team will be using Google Groups. In this section, we will walk through the different options and how to choose the right combination for your organization:

Sharing settings

Set policies that control public access to groups, who can create a group, and group visibility in the groups directory.

Sharing options

Sharing options allow you to define who can create, use, see, and manage the groups created in a domain:

Outside this domain - access to groups
Select the highest level of access to your groups for users outside this domain:

○ **Public on the Internet** - Anyone on the Internet can view, search, and post to groups
◉ **Private** - No one outside of the domain can view or search in groups, but external users may email the group if the group settings allow

---

The first section will allow you to define the default access to groups for people outside the organization. If you select **Public on the Internet**, anyone will be able to view, search, and post on the groups, which is great for interacting with customers and building a community around a product or service. Selecting **Private** will restrict access to people within the organization only—external users would require an invitation.

Default View Topics permission

Within a group, there are usually many discussion topics. The **Default View Topics permission** allow you to define the default level of view access for users according to their role, which can be owner, manager, member, or anyone:

Default View Topics permission
Select the default View Topics permission for groups created in Groups for Business:

○ Owners only
○ Owners and managers
○ All members of the group
◉ All users in the domain
○ Anyone on the Internet

In some cases, you might want to restrict access to the topics lists of a channel. **Owners only** will make it so that only the owners of the channel can see the topics list, while using **Owners and managers** will also allow managers to see it. **All members of the group** will only allow members to read the full topics list, and **Anyone on the internet** will open it up to the general public.

Creating groups

You should define who can create groups inside your domain. By default, this is set to **Anyone in this domain can create groups**, which allows anyone with an account in this domain to create groups:

Creating groups

◯ Anyone on the Internet can create groups (Available only if 'Public on the Internet' is selected)
⦿ Anyone in this domain can create groups
◯ Only domain admins can create groups

☐ Add a suffix to groups created by users: **group-name**   @cesarstechinsights.net

But you can also make it more restrictive with **Only domain admins can create groups**, or you can make this an open forum and enable **Anyone on the Internet** to create them.

Optionally, you can automatically add a suffix to the name of groups created by users; this can be anything you wish.

Member and email access

In some cases, you may wish to invite people from outside the organization to join or send messages to a private group. You can set permissions to **Group owners can allow members from outside this domain**, which will allow clients and other people from outside the organization to be invited to join certain discussions. You can also set a permission to **Group owners can allow incoming email from outside this domain**, which allows clients to use the group's email address to send messages. This is great for customer support:

Member & email access

☐ Group owners can allow members from outside this domain
        Domain admins can always add members from outside this domain

☐ Group owners can allow incoming email from outside this domain

It's recommended to create a group called Support that can only be seen by managers and owners, and set your support team as managers of this group. This allows people to send messages to support@yourorganization.com and only the support team will be able to see them.

Group visibility

In some cases, you may want to give the group owners the ability to hide certain groups from the domain's groups directory. When you enable this, you can also set it to **Hide newly created groups from the groups directory** by default:

Group visibility

☐ Group owners can hide groups from the groups directory
☐ Hide newly created groups from the groups directory

Consider this if your team usually creates new groups to discuss confidential matters or for customer engagement.

Uninstalling services

You can fully disable Groups by using the **Uninstall Groups for Business** option. This will make all of Groups' contents inaccessible to everyone, but the information will be kept and can be restored by reinstalling the service:

Uninstall Groups for Business
You can uninstall and remove this service without losing any data.

If you uninstall Groups and later wish to bring it back, take these steps from the administrator home:

1. Select **Apps**
2. Click on **G Suite**
3. Click on **ADD SERVICES**
4. Find **Groups for Business** in the **Already Purchased Services** section and click **ADD IT NOW:**

You can use these same steps to reinstall other G Suite services, and also to add more features in the **Additional Paid Services** and the **Other Services** sections.

Team engagement with G+ for Business

Internet users today spend a lot of time on social media. This can be considered negative inside the workplace, but Google+ for Business allows you to create a dedicated social media portal for your business that can be adjusted to be very useful for a team.

These groups can be private or public depending on the nature of what is being discussed. It's a great place for teams to share and discuss ideas, projects, and news, and also provides a place for members to get to know each other, even in large teams.

To find the G+ settings, take these steps from the administrator home page:

1. Select **Apps**
2. Click on **G Suite**
3. Select **Google+**

Advanced settings

G+ can block external access to the domain's communities, enforce age restrictions, allow or block a user's profile from being visible to search engines, and allow integration with third-party apps and the sending of external invitations:

> Advanced settings
>
> Set sharing policies and default settings for profiles, posts and hangouts.

Let's explore how to apply these settings.

Content Sharing and Access

The **Content Sharing and Access** settings allow you to define the community's external visibility:

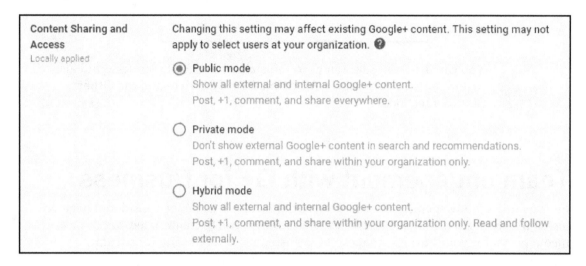

- Selecting **Public mode** allows anyone to post, +1, and share freely
- **Private mode** keeps everything private within the organization
- **Hybrid mode** only allows members of the organization to use the platform, but external users can read and follow the content, so this is useful for posting notifications to your clients

Sharing posts

The **Sharing posts** section allows you to restrict the sharing of content outside the organization:

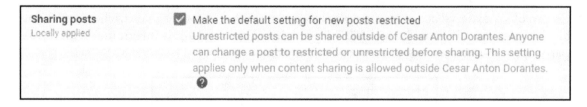

The default setting for new posts is **restricted**, although users may manually choose to allow them to be shared outside the organization if **Content Sharing and Access** is set to **Public mode** or **Hybrid mode**.

Profile discoverability

Enabling **Profile discoverability** will make the team's user profiles available to the public through search engines by default, but members or the organization can choose to make their profiles private manually:

Profile discoverability
Locally applied

☐ Help people outside of Cesar Anton Dorantes find user profiles in search results

This configures the default profile discoverability setting for users in Cesar Anton Dorantes. Any user can change their personal discoverability settings from this default. This setting applies only when content sharing is allowed outside Cesar Anton Dorantes. ❓

Profile creation

Enabling **Profile creation** will automatically generate G+ profiles for all members of the organization:

Profile creation
Locally applied

☐ Automatically create Google+ profiles

By checking this box, you certify that all users in this organization are 18 or older. Do not check this box if any users in this organization may be under 18. You are solely responsible for compliance with laws and regulations that apply to the provision of Google+ to end users, including the Children's Online Privacy Protection Act of 1998 where applicable. If you are a reseller you are responsible for informing the customer of this information prior to enabling this feature. ❓

Keep in mind that you should not enable this if there are members who are less than 18 years old. If that is the case, you need to put all underage members into a separate organizational unit with this option disabled for them.

Profiles

Administrators can use the **Profiles** section to quickly search and review all profiles for the members of this domain:

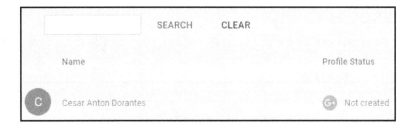

Communicating via Hangouts Chat and Meet

Video conferences are a very popular way to communicate, and Hangouts Meet offers convenient solutions, from direct video conferences to online meetings and presentations of up to 50 members for Business accounts, or up to 100 for Enterprise users.

Meet also offers the ability to join meetings via phone, and also for the organizer to call someone to join the meeting, all in a very simple and intuitive way. Alternative solutions, such as **Cisco WebEx**, are more expensive, harder to use, and are not always reliable.

Google Hangouts

To find the Hangouts settings, take these steps from the administrator homepage:

1. Select **Apps**
2. Click on **G Suite**
3. Select **Google Hangouts**

Chat settings

You can enable **Chat | History** so that users can store conversation logs in their Gmail accounts so that they can review them later, if needed:

Chat
Locally applied

Some features of classic Hangouts, like photo sharing, may require other Google services to be enabled. ❷

History ❷

For all classic Hangouts conversations:

- ⦿ History is on
- ◯ History is off

☐ Don't allow users to change this setting.

Google Hangouts allows users to find and talk with anyone outside the organization who has a Google account. In **Sharing options**, you can choose whether external users can see a member's status to see whether they are available. It's recommended to enable the option to warn users when having a Hangout outside the organization:

Sharing options
Locally applied

Chatting outside this organization (Within the Google network) ❷

Users can automatically chat with other G Suite and Gmail users (Google network)

- ☑ Display users' chat status outside Cesar Anton Dorantes
- ☑ Warn users when having a Hangout outside Cesar Anton Dorantes ❷
- ☑ Users can chat with other users outside Cesar Anton Dorantes

Administrators can make it so that **Chat invitations** between members of the domain are accepted automatically:

Chat invitations
Locally applied

☐ Automatically accept invitations between users within Cesar Anton Dorantes

Meet settings

Hangouts Meet allows members of your organization to use more advanced features than the ones typically available for Hangouts users in meetings of up to 25 connections for Basic and Business accounts, and 50 for Enterprise users. Considering that a meeting room would count as just one connection, you could connect many offices and a few members that are working remotely.

Enable **Dial-in** and Hangouts Meet automatically creates a phone number and PIN for each video meeting so that users can join through a phone call.

Hangouts Chat

Hangouts Chat provides a safe and convenient way for members of your organization to send written messages to other users, groups, or even virtual rooms with a capacity of up to 8,000 members dedicated to a single project or topic.

To find Chat settings, take these steps from the administrator homepage:

1. Select **Apps**
2. Click on **G Suite**
3. Select **Hangouts Chat**

The **History Settings** page allows you to set chat history storage to **ON** or **OFF** by default, but allows users to change it for their own account. Alternatively, you can also enforce the same policy for everyone so that users cannot change it:

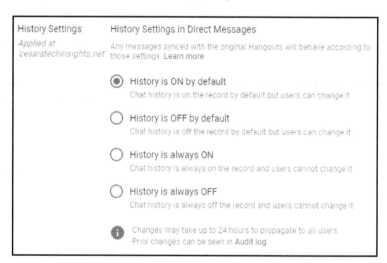

In the **Bots** settings, you can allow users to install and use bots. Depending on the G Suite Marketplace settings for this domain, users may be able to use any bot, or may be limited to a previously approved list:

Hangouts will be at the core of users' real-time communications. In the next section, you will learn about Google Drive, which will be at the core of users' real-time collaborations.

Understanding Google Drive

Google Drive is a safe, practical, and scalable solution for storing, sharing, and collaborating on files with other people. Teams and individuals can safely store their information and make it immediately accessible to others, from the entire world to just members of a list of up to 200 groups or accounts.

Google Docs is a cloud office suit that is built on top of Google Drive and is designed to work directly on a web browser, so there is no need to install additional software or plugins. It has some useful features, such as saving changes in real time to prevent losing work, automatically generating change logs to easily review and roll back changes, and allowing real-time collaboration on the same document with up to 100 simultaneous collaborators.

One important difference between regular Google Drive and the G Suite version is that everything that happens creates a log, so administrators can review a log file that includes changes, views, shares, and even prints.

To find the Drive settings, take these steps from the administrator homepage:

1. Select **Apps**
2. Click on **G Suite**
3. Select **Drive and Docs**

Sharing settings

Administrators should define the limitations for sharing Google Drive documents, maps, and folders outside the organization.

Sharing options

Sharing outside of your organization can be turned **OFF** to avoid data being shared with or seen by third parties. You can also limit sharing to a list of whitelisted domains, or leave it **ON** so that users can freely share files with other people. When sharing is off or limited, you can additionally allow or block users from receiving files from outside the organization to prevent, for example, users from receiving viruses. You can set Drive to warn when sharing with users outside the domain, even if they are whitelisted. It's possible to allow users without a Google account to access shared files, but it's best to only use this for completely public information.

Access Checker allows you to tell the system how to handle sharing when a file is shared using Google products other than the Docs interface, by showing users the options available for sharing content outside the organization:

Access Checker

When a user shares a file via a Google product other than Docs or Drive (e.g. by pasting a link in Gmail), Google can check that the recipients have access. If not, when possible, Google will ask the user to pick if they want to share the file to:

- ◉ Recipients only, Cesar Anton Dorantes, or public (no Google account required).
- ◯ Recipients only, or Cesar Anton Dorantes.
- ◯ Recipients only.

Team Drive creation

Team Drives provide members of an organization a shared space to work. This has the advantage that the files belong to the team, so files remain in place even if members leave. As an administrator, you have the following options for Team Drive creation—enable the ones that best suit your needs:

- **Prevent users from creating new Team Drives**: Only administrators can create new Team Drives
- **Prevent full-access members from modifying Team Drive settings**: Only administrators can change Team Drive settings

- **Prevent people outside the organization from accessing files in the Team Drive**: Team Drive is only accessible to members of the organization
- **Prevent non-members of the Team Drive from accessing files in the Team Drive**: Use and access is restricted to members
- **Prevent commenters and viewers from downloading, copying and printing files in the Team Drive**: Non-collaborators with access can't download, copy, or print the contents

Link sharing

You can set the default **Link Sharing** options for new files to **OFF**, accessible to anyone in the organization, or to just those with the link.

Migration settings

Administrators can **Allow users to migrate files to Team Drives**, or in other words, transfer ownership so that others can collaborate and ensure work will continue even if a user leaves the organization. Once enabled, the owner of a file can migrate a file to a Team Drive that they are a member of.

Transferring ownership

Administrators can manually transfer ownership from one member of an organization to another by simply typing in their accounts and clicking on **TRANSFER FILES**:

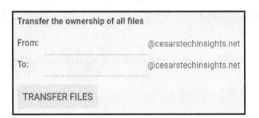

Features and Applications

The **Features and Applications** section allows administrators to define whether users can use add-ons, enable external app integration, and be able to create local backups of files on their devices.

Offline setting

The **Offline setting** is **Allow users to enable offline access** by default, but you can choose to **Control offline access using device policies** if you wish to restrict this option to previously authorized devices to prevent sensitive data from potential leaks.

Drive File Stream settings

If you **Allow Drive File Stream in your organization**, users will be able to use files in their machines straight from the cloud—in other words, without actually downloading them. Drive File Stream can integrate with Microsoft Office files so users can see in real time if other users are editing a certain file, although administrators can choose to disable this feature.

Drive settings

For an even deeper offline integration, Drive offers an installable desktop version, so users can keep a local copy of files on their machines and any changes done to them will sync automatically next time the software detects internet connectivity. It's possible to disable this feature, or to keep it enabled but hide the download links so that users can only use it via Google Drive to avoid potential security problems.

Drive SDK

Enabling the **Drive SDK** will allow third-party apps to integrate with the domain's Drive. The Drive SDK includes libraries and examples for the web and Android. It is built around the Google Drive API and is meant to facilitate creating systems that integrate with Google Drive.

Your team can use the Drive SDK to create custom systems that extend the functionality of Drive to better fit the team's particular needs. We will explore how to easily create custom software when we talk about creating sites and getting started with App Maker.

Templates

We enable **Templates** so that the members of an organization can choose or create shared templates to give Docs, Sheets, Forms, and Slides files a standardized appearance:

Enable custom templates for your organization
Allow users in your organization to find and use organization-specific templates from the Docs, Sheets, Slides, and Forms home screens

In the **Template submission** settings, you can define who can submit templates to the organization's library by choosing one of the following options:

- **Open**: This allows everyone in the organization to submit templates, which works great for small and new teams.
- **Moderated**: This also allows everyone in the organization to submit templates, but they must be approved by an administrator before they are added to the shared library.
- **Restricted**: This only allows administrators to submit templates. It's recommended for large teams.

Templates come in different categories. Administrators can choose which categories will be made available for selection in the library simply by selecting or creating the ones they need:

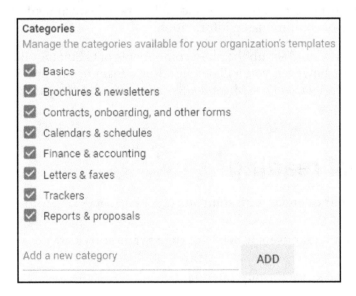

Summary

In this chapter, we learned how to set up an organization's Calendar, starting with sharing events and availability between members and the public, setting up resources to make choosing the right location easier for users, and making and highlighting the most and least used resources. We also looked at how to integrate Calendar and Microsoft Exchange.

Now you know how to use Google Groups to group members of an organization and route messages, such as support requests, to the right people in the organization. You can now set up a dedicated social network so that your organization can help its members collaborate internally, or with their customers and partners.

In this chapter, you also got familiar with how to set up Google Hangouts Chat and Meet as an organization, along with how collaborators can use it to improve their real-time communication, while being aware of its limits.

Finally, we walked through Google Drive's configurations. We learned how to set up the configuration options, migrate documents between accounts, transfer ownership, and how to enable or block the offline features of the service. With Google Drive, members of an organization can create, edit, store, share, and collaborate on documents, without having to worry about losing or compromising information.

By now, you can create and set up the main components of G Suite for Business for a new domain. Sometimes, however, you will be migrating a team from a previous system, so in Chapter 4, *Moving on with Data Migration Systems*, we will focus on the details of dealing with legacy services.

Additional reading

- **Share your calendar with someone** (https://support.google.com/calendar/answer/37082#permissions)
- **Allow Calendar users to see Exchange availability data** (https://support.google.com/a/answer/7437483?hl=en)
- **Create and share a group calendar** (https://support.google.com/a/answer/1626902?hl=en)
- **Get started with Calendar Interop** (https://support.google.com/a/answer/7441020?hl=enref_topic=7437779)
- **Integrating Outlook and Exchange with G Suite** (https://support.google.com/a/answer/33322?hl=en)

Moving On with Data Migration Services

4

G Suite gives organizations and professionals the tools they need to have safe and reliable communication and collaboration. Some of them are lucky enough to get it from day one, but in many cases, the organization might be using a certain version of Microsoft Office and they will need you to help them migrate.

Free Google accounts offer a wide range of solutions, so it's not rare to see users and businesses using the free version, but then looking to upgrade to G Suite at some point, if at the least to get a custom domain name.

Even if Google accounts are the most popular choice for personal accounts, Microsoft has been around for longer. Therefore, corporations are more familiar with it and many have been using it for many years, and changing to something different is a big step for them. As a G Suite administrator, it's your duty to make the transition smooth and ensure that things just keep working and no information is lost.

In this chapter, we will learn how to migrate emails between G Suite and external Gmail accounts, as well as from Microsoft Exchange, Microsoft Office 365, or webmail providers using an **Internet Message Access Protocol** (**IMAP**) like Yahoo or iCloud.

We will see how to integrate G Suite with Microsoft Exchange accounts so that members of the organization can use both services to have a smooth transition between systems.

As an administrator, you will also learn how to migrate emails, calendar events, and contacts information from Microsoft Exchange accounts and other sources, like Hotmail or Yahoo, into G Suite.

Be ready to learn the steps and best practices to migrate all of this information so that when we finish this chapter, you know how to do the following:

- Identify the requirements for successful migration of corporate emails, contacts, and calendars
- Perform email migrations from other service providers
- Perform contacts migrations from other service providers
- Perform calendar events migrations from other service providers
- Integrate G Suite with existing Microsoft Exchange accounts

We will start by learning how to manage email, contacts, and calendar events.

Managing migrations

As a G Suite administrator, one of your roles is to help users in your organization migrate from a legacy system to G Suite.

Migrations are also necessary when the organization needs to move from one G Suite account to another. When large organizations decide to split into different branches, you will find yourself needing to target specific users during the migration.

In this section, we will learn how to use the **Data Migration** tool of the administrator home page to perform migrations for emails, contacts, and calendar events.

To get to the migration tools from the administrator home page, follow these steps:

1. Click on **Data Migration**
2. Select **What would you like to migrate?**

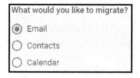

You can select **Email**, **Contacts**, or **Calendar**. There are some key differences between each kind of migration, so we will explore each option in its own section.

Once you create a migration session this steps will not apply, close your existing session to reset the migration flow.

Our first step will be to learn how to perform email migrations from legacy servers in *Managing Email migrations*.

Managing email migrations

Gmail has grown a lot in popularity, not only because it's free and easy to use, but also because it's integrated with other popular services like YouTube, as well as Android devices. Gmail has reached one billion users since 2016 and that grew to 1.5 billion by 2018.

Not everyone that uses email is using Gmail, so let's learn how to help them move from whatever they are using to Gmail.

Setting up an email migration source

The **Migration source** settings hold the information that G Suite requires to connect to the server that holds the accounts that we need to migrate, as well as the necessary credentials to access the information.

Before we can start migrating messages, we need to learn how to set up the migration source. To do that, follow these steps:

1. Go to the migration tools page; you can find the steps at the beginning of this chapter.
2. Select **Email** and click **CONTINUE.**
3. Select **Migration source**. Now, it's time to tell Gmail about the IMAP server we are migrating from:

Migration source	Select the type of mail server you are migrating from. If you don't know or are unsure, select 'I dont know / Other IMAP server'.

Most of the migration sources will work in a similar fashion, but there are key differences, depending on where you are migrating from. Let's explore the different options:

- **Gmail:** After you select it, all other options will go away:
    1. Click **CONNECT**
    2. Proceed to the next section, *Migrating messages*

- **G Suite**, **GoDaddy**, **Microsoft Exchange 2003**, **Microsoft Exchange 2007**, **Microsoft Exchange 20010**, **Microsoft Exchange 2013/2016** or **Microsoft Office 365**:
  1. Verify that you have **Auto select** as the **Connection protocol**:

  2. Type the role account credentials in this section, as shown in the following screenshot:

  3. Click **CONNECT**
  4. Proceed to the next section, *Migrating messages*

- **I dont know / Other IMAP server:** There are cases where you might want to move emails from service providers that work with IMAP, like Yahoo or iCloud. You need to have an account name and password that can access these accounts:
  1. Select **IMAP** as the **Connection protocol**.
  2. Write the **IMAP Server Name** and port, for example:

    - For **Outlook**, use `http://outlook.office365.com:995`
    - For **Yahoo**, use `http://imap.mail.yahoo.com:993`
    - For **iCloud**, use `imap.mail.me.com:993`

3. Type in the **Role account** credentials. For corporate accounts, we can save a lot of time by using a single account with access privileges to all of the accounts we will migrate from that particular domain:

admin@domain.com

Password

4. Click **CONNECT**

Always remember to get the role account credentials before you start any migration.

 With the exception of Gmail, you need to be able to provide the login credentials of an account that can access the old email. For personal accounts, this is the credentials for that account, and for business accounts, it's best to have a single administrator's account that can access all of the accounts that will be migrated.

Now that we have made a bridge between both servers, let's proceed to learn how to perform the actual migration.

Migrating messages

Once we have set up our source, it's time to start performing the actual migration; we will start by defining what we want to migrate. At the top of the form, you will see the **Migration start date**, and it will have a drop-down menu that will allow you to define from what date to start migrating your messages, as shown here:

Migration start date	Select start date for migration. We will migrate your email from that date to the most recent, starting with the most recent first.
	Past 1 year ▾

With **Migration options**, you can define if you also wish to **Migrate deleted email**, **Migrate junk email**, or if you wish to exclude top-level folders from migration by providing a comma-separated list of the folder names:

Migration options	Choose migration options as you need.
	☐ Migrate deleted email
	☐ Migrate junk email
	☐ Exclude following top level folders from migration (comma separated list)

To start the migration process, click on **Select user** to open the **Start Email Migration** flow:

Data migration > Email

Name	IMAP email (From)	G Suite email (To)	Status

No migration in progress. Click on the start button below to select user(s) and start migration.

On the left, you will place the email that will be **Migrate From**, and on the right, the account that will be **Migrate To**, as shown in the following screenshot:

Migrate From:		Migrate To:
Gmail Email address	AUTHORIZE	Start typing and select from list
Authorization Code		

If you are coming from Gmail or another G Suite account, after writing the source address on the **Migrate From** field, you need to click on **AUTHORIZE** to open a new tab with the **G Suite Data Migration Service** authorization, where you must log in to this account and click on **Allow** on the confirmation window:

Sign in

to continue to G Suite Data Migration Service

Email or phone

G Suite Data Migration Service wants to access your Google Account

 reicek@gmail.com

This will allow G Suite Data Migration Service **to:**

Ⓜ Read, compose, send, and permanently delete all ⓘ your email from Gmail

Once you allow the data migration service to have access to your account, it will give you a code that you should copy and paste on the **Authorization Code** field of the **Migrate From** section:

Google

Sign in

Please copy this code, switch to your application and paste it there:

Migrate From:

Gmail Email address

Authorization Code

Now that we have the origin set up, make sure that you have chosen the account that the messages will be sent to. This must be within the organization, and once you are ready, click **START**. Congratulations! The migration is in process and you will be able to see the migration process status on the list. Note that the list is not in real time, so you need to refresh the site to see its progress:

If needed, you can stop an ongoing migration by clicking on the options icon on the right and selecting **Stop Migration**, as shown at the bottom of the following screenshot:

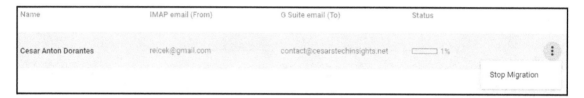

Proceed to the next section to learn how migration works for contacts.

Managing contacts migration

Businesses usually have many partners and key clients they keep in touch with, and during a migration, it's important to be able to move them into the new account.

In this section, we will explore how to migrate from Gmail, G Suite, Microsoft Exchange, and IMAP servers in general.

Setting up a contacts migration source

To be able to migrate contacts from one account to another, you also need to set up a migration source.

To get to the contacts migration tool from the administrator home page, follow these steps:

1. Go to the migration tools page; you can find the steps at the beginning of this chapter.
2. Click on **Data Migration**.
3. Select **Contacts**.
4. Click **CONTINUE**.
5. Select **Migration source**. Select the kind of server you are migrating from. If you are not migrating from an Exchange server, don't worry—you will learn how to do that when we talk about importing a contacts file. If it's not on the list, or you are not sure, select **I dont know / Other Exchange server.**
6. Validate that the **Connection protocol** is set to **Auto Select**.
7. Type the role account that will be used for the migration. This account must have impersonation rights for all the accounts that will be migrated so that it can access and relay the contacts information.
8. Click **CONNECT.**
9. Click **SELECT USERS**, as shown in the following screenshot:

Connection successful! You are almost done.

In the next step you can select users* and migrate their contacts.

CANCEL   SELECT USERS

Now, you will be taken to the **Contacts Data Migration** tool. In the next section, we will explore how to use it.

Migrating contacts

Contacts migration is very similar to what we learned for emails. In the **Contacts Data Migration** tool, you will see a list of the current migrations in progress, or start new ones.

To start a migration, follow these steps:

1. Hover over 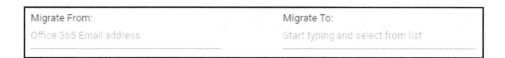 and select the kind of migration you need:
   - **Select multiple users**: Use this when you need to migrate multiple accounts:
     1. Click **ATTACH FILE**. Provide a CSV file with the format `<new G Suite email>, <previous email>`.
     2. Click **UPLOAD AND START MIGRATION**.
   - **Select user**: Use this when you are migrating a single account:
     1. Type the old email on **Migrate From**
     2. Type the new email on **Migrate To**
     3. Click **START**

Migrate From:	Migrate To:
Office 365 Email address	Start typing and select from list

Your transfers will now show on the **Data migration > Contacts** table, as shown in the following screenshot:

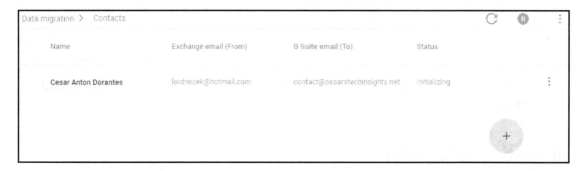

If you need to stop an ongoing transfer, click on the Options icon at the far right of that migration row.

Migrating contacts using server to server communication is very useful when migrating from a compatible server, but you can also use files to import contacts. Let's learn how this works in the next section.

Importing and exporting a contacts file

When our sources are not migrating from a Microsoft Exchange server, the users will have to import their contacts manually using a CSV file. However, this is a very easy operation.

Migrating contacts using files has the advantage that you can use the files as a backup for your contacts.

While migrating from another Google account, users need to go to their source account, and on the left menu toggle **More** and click on **Export contacts**, as shown in the following screenshot:

A Google CSV contacts file has the following structure:

```
Name,Given Name,Additional Name,Family Name,Yomi
Name,Given Name Yomi,Additional Name Yomi,Family Name
Yomi,Name Prefix,Name Suffix,Initials,Nickname,Short
Name,Maiden Name,Birthday,Gender,Location,Billing
Information,Directory
Server,Mileage,Occupation,Hobby,Sensitivity,Priority,Subj
ect,Notes,Language,Photo,Group Membership,E-mail 1 -
Type,E-mail 1 - Value,E-mail 2 - Type,E-mail 2 -
Value,Phone 1 - Type,Phone 1 - Value,Phone 2 - Type,Phone
2 - Value,Website 1 - Type,Website 1 - Value
```

To import a contacts CSV or vCard file, users need to observe the following steps:

1. Open the **Contacts** account in this domain.
2. Toggle **More** on the left menu.
3. Click on **Import contacts**. You will see the **Import contacts** form, as shown in the following screenshot:

4. Click **Select file** and load the file with the contacts information. When a file is loaded, the name will show up next to the **Select file** button.
5. Click **Import** to move the contacts. You will see an **All done** notification, and all the contacts will now be in the system:

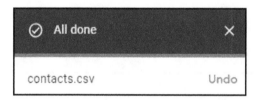

Now that you can import contacts using server to server communication, and also import users contacts manually using files, it's time to learn how to migrate calendar events in the next section.

Managing calendar migration

So far, we have learned how to migrate emails and contacts. Now, it's time to learn how to migrate calendars into G Suite; after this, you will be able to identify the right tool, depending on where are you migrating from, as well as the necessary steps to do it successfully.

Setting up a calendar migration source

To get to the calendar migration tool, from the administrator home page, follow these steps:

1. Go to the migration tools page; you can find the steps at the beginning of this chapter.
2. Click on **Data Migration**.
3. Select **Calendar** and click **CONTINUE**.
4. Choose the **Migration source** that works best for you. If you are not sure, select **I dont know / Other IMAP server**.
5. Verify you have **Auto select** as the **Connection protocol**, as shown here:

6. Type the **Role account** credentials, as shown in the following screenshot:

7. Click **CONNECT**.

Now that we have configured our migration source, we can proceed to migrate events to the new account. In the next section, we will learn how to do this.

Migrating events

To migrate events, follow these steps:

1. **Select the Migration start date**: This will tell the system how far back it should go during the event's import process. It can be the **Past month**, **3 months**, **6 months** or **1 year**:

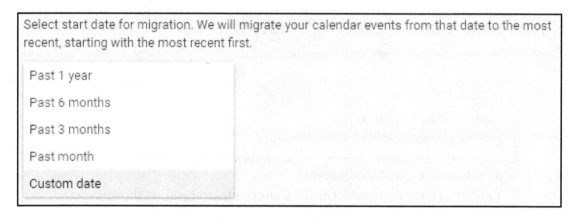

Alternatively, you can select since a **Custom date**, as shown in the following screenshot:

2. **Migration options**: This gives you the option to also migrate secondary calendar events together with the main calendar:

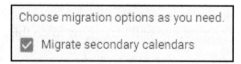

3. **User Mapping**: Enable this for migrating multiple accounts. This allows you to provide a CSV file with a list of addresses, using the new address as the first, the old one as the second, and an optional third parameter for the password on the old account, which is needed, unless you are migrating from Gmail, Microsoft Exchange, or Microsoft Office 365:

 Email address changed for one or more users.

Please upload a comma separated value (CSV) file for only those users who have email addresses in the source system different from their G Suite email address. Also include any resource calendars that need to be migrated.

In order to help you create the file, you can download all the users in your G Suite account from the users page.

Please use the following format:
<G Suite email id>, <Source email address>

Please note:
A mapping entry in the file is needed only for users whose source email address is different from G Suite email address. We recommend that you include all such users even if you are not migrating any of them because they may appear as participants in others' meetings. Include all calendar resources, if any.

Examples:
joe@yourgoogledomain.com,bob@olddomain.com
newname@yourgoogledomain.com,oldname@olddomain.com

 ATTACH FILE

Up until now, we have focused on using the G Suite administrator's home page, but G Suite also provides specialized migration tools that can help us with certain cases. We'll learn more about this in the next section.

Migration tools

Google provides a series of tools that facilitates migrating calendar information into the system, depending on where the data is coming from, so let's explore the different solutions.

If your users are migrating from Microsoft Exchange, ask them to download and install the **G Suite Migration for Microsoft® Exchange (GSMME)** tool from `https://tools.google.com/dlpage/exchangemigration` at the computer they normally use to access their account.

For those coming from Microsoft Outlook, they need to download and install the **G Suite Migration for Microsoft Outlook® (GSMMO)** tool instead from `https://tools.google.com/dlpage/outlookmigration` at the computer they are migrating the data from.

There is also a tool for migrating from IBM Notes using the **G Suite Migration for IBM® Notes® (GSMIN)** tool, which can be downloaded from `https://support.google.com/a/answer/154630`, where they usually access their IBM Notes data.

Once installed, they can follow these steps:

1. Run **G Suite Migration for Microsoft Outlook** from the start menu. They will see the following screen:

2. Type your **Email address**.
3. Click **Continue**. Your web browser will be launched, and a new tab will be open on the Google sign in site.
4. Click on the account you wish to use or log into a different one by clicking **Use another account**:

5. You will be shown a large list of permissions that are required by the app. Click **Allow**, as shown at the bottom right of the following screenshot:

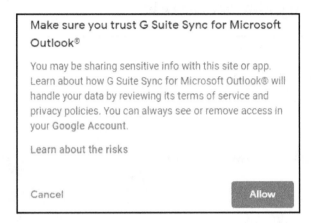

6. Select the account you wish to migrate to:

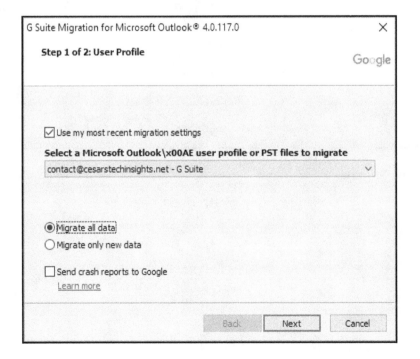

7. Select if you wish to **Migrate all data** or **Migrate only new data**.
8. Click **Next**.
9. Select what you wish to be migrated:

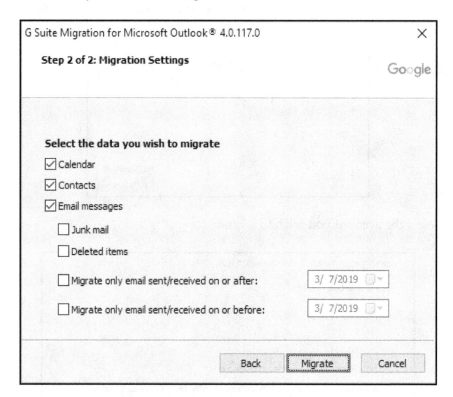

10. Click **Migrate**.

11. Wait until all migrations are ready:

12. Once the migrations are over, click **OK** to close the tool, as shown in the following screenshot:

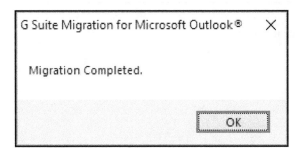

This tool is most commonly used in corporate environments that has a Windows for Business edition and Microsoft Outlook or Microsoft Exchange installed as a legacy system. You should collaborate with the Windows administrator of the organization to help you install the migration tool safely for all users.

Integrating with Microsoft services

Many large corporations use Microsoft Exchange, and sometimes, they don't want to fully let go of their systems, or they need to be able to use it in combination with G Suite as part of the transition process. In this chapter, we will explore how we can integrate with Microsoft Outlook and Microsoft Exchange.

The first step for your users is to install and set up GSSMO for sync from `https://tools.google.com/dlpage/gappssync` and run it. The app will ask the user to log in to their G Suite account and to authorize access to their account information by clicking **Allow**:

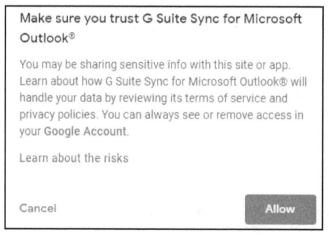

Once they have given access, GSSMO will give the user the option to import their data. Here, they can select what elements to migrate before syncing. Once they've made their selections, they need to click **Create profile** and then **Start Microsoft Outlook®** to finish the setup:

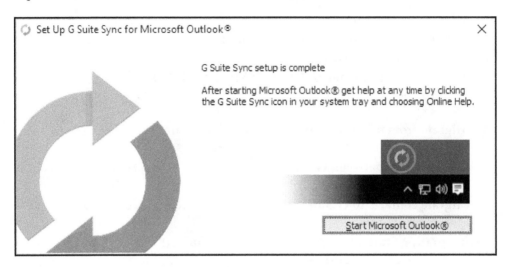

From now on, you can help the users in your domains to synchronize with Outlook. Again, it is advised to do this in collaboration with the Windows administrator to install these tools safely on all authorized computers.

Summary

Congratulations! You now know the main options for performing email migration from Microsoft Exchange, Microsoft Outlook, an IMAP server, a free Google account, or another G Suite domain. With this, you have the necessary knowledge to help a team move from Microsoft services into G Suite.

We walked through the different ways in which we can perform migrations for calendar events, contacts, and emails from different systems, so you can now identify the differences and similarities between the different migration sources and options.

Finally, we learned where to get and how to set up the specialized tools that the G Suite team made to allows users to migrate and integrate G Suite and Microsoft Outlook or Microsoft Exchange, so that teams can have a smooth transition between systems.

In the next chapter, we will learn about managing multiple domains and user accounts.

Further reading

- **Migrate from Gmail to G Suite** (https://support.google.com/a/answer/6167866?hl=enref_topic=6351498)
- **Migration terms to know** (https://support.google.com/a/answer/7001020)
- **Migrate email from one G Suite account to another** (https://support.google.com/a/answer/6351475?hl=en)
- **Migrate from Exchange or Office 365 to G Suite** (https://support.google.com/a/answer/180898?hl=enref_topic=6351498visit_id=636878868873810593-3377032471rd=1)
- **Migrate from other webmail providers to G Suite** (https://support.google.com/a/answer/6351474?hl=enref_topic=6351498)
- **Transfer data between G Suite accounts** (https://support.google.com/a/answer/1041297?hl=en)
- **Migrate contacts to G Suite** (https://support.google.com/a/answer/6174025?hl=en)
- **Integrating Outlook and Exchange with G Suite** (https://support.google.com/a/answer/33322?hl=en)
- **Administrator setup for GSMMO** (https://support.google.com/a/answer/176213)
- **About synchronizing G Suite with Outlook** (https://support.google.com/a/users/answer/153866?hl=en)

Section 2: G Suite with Google Domains 2

In this section, you will learn how to complete the advanced setup of additional business domains and how to administrate users in multiple domains.

The following chapters are included in this section:

- Chapter 5, *Setting Up Domains and Users*
- Chapter 6, *Monitoring Reports*
- Chapter 7, *Archiving with Vault*

5
Setting Up Domains and Users

Organizations may grow to a point where they need to divide into different branches or create special teams dedicated to an important project.

These teams may have their own domain and be able to collaborate and communicate using G Suite, but with their resources isolated from the rest of the organization. This also gives teams the ability to choose how much they want to share with the rest of the organization, and therefore, reduces potential security issues.

G Suite allows you to concentrate multiple domains into a single account or handle each domain as a separate account; this gives you great flexibility as an administrator when you need to manage several domains.

Managing multiple domains also means being able to add users and associate their accounts to the right domain or domains. You can choose to add users that are exclusive to a single domain or make accounts work for all domains using something called a domain alias.

In this chapter, we will explore how to set up additional domains, and how to administrate users in these multiple domains scenarios.

You will learn about the following topics:

- Getting additional domains using Google Domains
- Associating multiple domains for integrated teams
- Creating independent domains for modular teams
- Creating single or multiple user accounts
- Administering user accounts across multiple domains

Adding a new domain

Adding new domains is very useful for businesses when they need to handle multiple brands. The way they need to distribute their users will define how we create the user accounts and associate them within these domains.

In this section, we will learn how to add additional domains to a G Suite account or create aliases for the same domain. We will learn about the differences between both approaches as well.

We will also learn how to use Google Domains to easy add new domains, or aliases, to an account. Google Domains is a tool that launched in 2015 and will make things much easier for you as an administrator; when dealing with multiple domains, it allows you to find and buy new domains easily, as well as administer the ones you already own.

With Google Domains, you can do the following:

- Find and buy new domains
- Set your domain licenses to be renewed automatically
- Create a website for it with a few clicks
- Forward visitors to an already existing site
- Manage the DNS settings for this domain
- Assign up to 100 email aliases to forward messages to specific email accounts or even use a wildcard
- Add a new Google account to a domain

To facilitate future access to Google Domains you can create an app-like direct access for Google Domains using Google Chrome by following these steps:

1. Go to `https://domains.google/`
2. Click ⋮ on the menus icon at top-right corner of the browser
3. Click **More tools**, followed by a click on **Create shortcut...**
4. Edit the name if you wish
5. Click **Create**, as shown in the following screenshot:

Let's start by learning how to create a new domain for an existing G Suite account.

Getting a new domain

Domain names are the user friendly way to locate a particular part of the internet, and there are many ways to buy new domains. In this section, we will explore the use of Google Domains to easily buy and administer new domains.

Let's get started with Google Domains, and obtain a new domain by following these steps:

1. Go to `https://domains.google/`
2. Click on **MANAGE MY DOMAINS** on the top-right corner:

3. Click on **Get a new domain**, and the following screenshot should appear:

4. Write the domain you are looking for in the search field at the center of the screen:

5. Click the search icon. You will see a list of all available and unavailable addresses for that domain, as well as the price per year for each one:

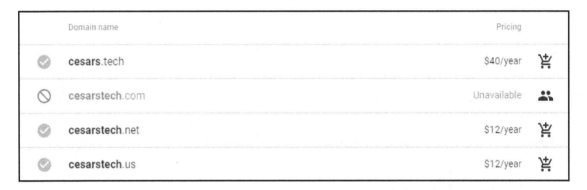

All domains must have what is known as the **Top-Level Domain** (**TLD**); these are the letters that follow the final dot on the address, and it is used to easily identify the purpose, for example, .org is used for organizations.

Before you can buy a domain, you must choose a top-level domain and, to make this task easier, you can apply some filters by clicking on the settings icon at the right of the domain search bar.

Clicking the **Availability** filter will toggle its state; when the setting is active, it will hide all of the domains that are already taken from the list:

By default, the list shows all possible top-level domains, but you can choose to only show the ones you are really interested in by selecting them from a list:

You can also hide all of the options that exceed a certain price limit:

When you see a domain you are interested in, just click on the icon next to its name to add it to the cart. You can add as many domains to the cart as you want:

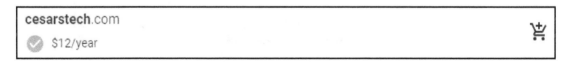

Once you have selected the domains you want, click on the cart icon to start the checkout.

We have a few options for our new domains; if you enable **Privacy protection**, your private information will not show under this domain in the **WHOIS** directory:

Enabling **Auto-renew** will automatically charge the renewal fee every year; this is important since it will prevent the domain accidentally becoming available to third parties. We can avoid a serious problem by leaving this enabled for the lifetime of this domain:

 Auto-renew is on

This domain will be auto-renewed around **January 22** every year. You will automatically be billed when the renewal occurs

Once you have selected your preferences, click **CHECKOUT** and you will see a contact information form; please fill it since it is required by ICANN. You can register the owner of the domain (**registrant**), the person responsible for the administrative decisions (**admin**), or the person responsible for technical changes on the domain (**tech**):

 Your information

Contact

This information is required by ICANN in order to reach you in case of problems with your registration. Learn more

Remember that, if you enable **Privacy protection**, the contact information will not be shown in the WHOIS directory. Once you are ready, click **SAVE & CONTINUE**:

 Review purchase

The **Review purchase** form will let you take one last look at your selections; make sure to double check that everything is in order, and once you are sure, click **BUY** and provide the information for the credit card to be charged for this domain.

We now have own a new domain; in the next section, we will learn how to use it with G Suite.

Domain aliases and additional domains

Now that we own at least one additional domain, it's time to associate it with the account; to do this, take these simple steps from the administrator home page:

1. Click **Domains** to go to the main domains management site.
2. Click **Add/remove domains** to go the the domains management table.
   Here you can add, remove, or deactivate additional domains and domain aliases. By default, you will see the main domain and a **Test domain alias**.
3. Click **ADD A DOMAIN OR A DOMAIN ALIAS.**
4. Select an option:
   - **Add a domain alias**: This will associate the new domain as an alias for the current primary domain of this account. This means that all members of the organization will get an email address for each registered domain, but all will be pointing to the same inbox folder. This is very useful when you have a single team handling multiple brands. You can associate up to 20 domain aliases for the primary domain, and there is no additional cost for a domain alias.

   - **Add another domain**: This will make the new domains independent from the primary domain of this account. You will have to add users separately for each new separate domain, and these will be charged independently. You can associate up to 599 separate domains into a single account. We will learn more about configuring non-primary domains in the next section.

5. Enter a domain alias.
6. Click **CONTINUE AND VERIFY DOMAIN OWNERSHIP**. This will confirm you own the domain. You don't need to worry about this if you acquired the domain directly from Google. If you didn't get the domain through Google, you have the following options:
   1. Select **Recommended method**: This will use special settings targeted for the most common domain name providers:
      1. Select the domain name provider you used to buy the domain
      2. Follow the instructions on screen for that domain

2. Select **Alternate methods**: These are generic approaches; use this if you can modify the code on the site, or request someone to do it for you. There are three options, however, you only need to use one:

   - **HTML tag**: This is a short piece of code that must be added to the home page.
   - **HTML file upload**: This is a small HTML file that you must add to the server and make accessible through a specific route.
   - **Google Analytics**: If this site uses Google Analytics, you can use that to confirm ownership. Keep in mind that you need to have access to the Google Analytics account used for this site.

Recommended method	Alternate methods

7. Click **VERIFY** to finish the setup. If you have trouble with verification, the **Alternate methods** are very reliable.

You can confirm whether a domain was correctly verified in the status column at the domains management table. You can also **REMOVE** or **DISABLE** additional domains and aliases by clicking the corresponding button, as shown in the following screenshot:

cesarstech.com	Verified. Set up Google MX records ✔ **Recommended** Or, Skip Google MX setup ❓ Rarely used	REMOVE

We just learned how to add new domains from within G Suite, but you can also do it from Google Domains; in the next section, you will learn how to do that.

Adding a new domain from Google Domains

Google Domains makes the task of adding and configuring new domains very easy; it's also very useful, since it provides a central tool to acquire and administer all of your domains.

To add a new domain using Google Domains, open a new browser tab and follow these steps:

1. Go to `https://domains.google.com`.
2. Click **Manage** on the domain you need, shown on the right-hand side of the following screenshot:

3. Click **GET G SUITE** on the **Get a custom email address** section, as shown in the following screenshot:

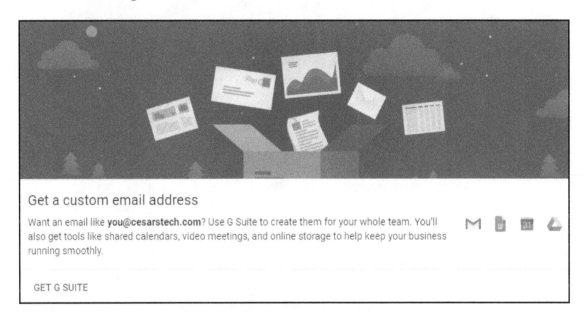

4. Click **NEXT** on the **Setup custom email with G Suite** form:

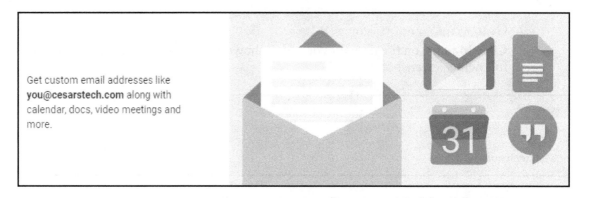

5. Click **Create admin user** account for this G Suite domain and provide a backup email address; I recommend using the address of the primary account administrator:

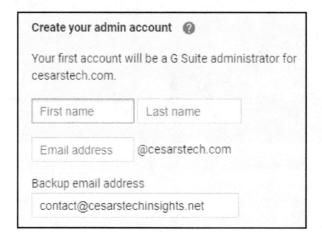

6. Choose one of the following plans: **G Suite Business** or **G Suite Basic**; if you are not sure, you can start with **G Suite Basic**, and upgrade later if you need a more robust plan:

G Suite Business $10.00 / user / month
Get custom emails, business tools, and added controls

- Includes everything from G Suite basic
- Unlimited cloud storage (or 1 TB/user if fewer than 5 users)
- Backup emails and chats indefinitely
- Added controls and reports to help protect your business

G Suite Basic $5.00 / user / month
Get custom emails and business tools

- Look professional with custom email addresses
- Get online tools like shared calendars, 30 GB of storage and video meetings

7. Click on **REVIEW YOUR PURCHASE.**

8. Choose or set up your payment method and click **BUY**:

contact@cesarstech.com
is now set up with G Suite.

Check your email to find your temporary password to log in to G Suite. You will need to change that password after you log in to your G Suite account.

And now you have a new G Suite account for a non-primary domain. If you are wondering about costs, there will be no charges until the next billing date, and the price will depend on how many user accounts we create for this domain.

You can now add additional domains to a G Suite account, but keep in mind that these non-primary domains have a few limitations, so let's explore the main ones in the next section.

Limitations with non-primary domains

When you associate additional domains to an account, they will have a few limitations. However, in most cases, they will make life easier for the administrator.

One limitation is that you are restricted to using one logo for all of your domains, usually the logo of the parent company.

It is important to keep in mind that domain aliases are only applied automatically when associated with the primary account. Separate domains may also use aliases, but these must be set up manually.

Google Drive sharing will be open for all primary and non-primary domain users. However, you can change this by assigning users to different organizational units.

You have learned how to buy new domains and use them as aliases for another domain, or as an additional non-primary domain. In the next section, we will learn how to add users to those accounts.

Administering user accounts in multiple domains

Managing multiple domains requires being able to add users to each domain independently. Even if you are handling several accounts, Google Domains and G Suite make it easy for you to go to the right domain and add or remove users, as needed.

A large business usually has different departments and teams that work independently of each other, even though they all form part of a larger parent company. As a Google administrator, one of your duties is to help these organizations be able to divide users into the different teams in an efficient way.

Switching between administrator accounts

As an administrator of multiple domains, you will find yourself jumping between different administrator accounts in order to access their associated G Suite administrator pages.

To change between administrator accounts, follow these steps from the admin page:

1. Click on the user picture in the top right-hand corner of the screen.
2. Click on the account that manages the domain you wish to manage. A new browser tab will open; this is the G Suite admin page of the selected account:

3. If the account is not on the list, click on **Add account** and log in to the administrator's account of that domain.

In the next section, we will learn how to add user accounts for a particular domain.

Adding users with G Suite

Adding new users is one of the most basic tasks of a G Suite administrator. Keep in mind that the cost of a domain is mostly determined by the number of user accounts in it.

To add a new user, follow these steps:

1. Validate you are using the administrator account in the domain where you want the new user to be.
2. Go to the administrator home page.
3. Click on the **Users** icon:

4. Hover over the yellow + icon, and click on one of the following:

- Click **Add new user** to create a single additional account:
    1. Upload a profile picture for the account:

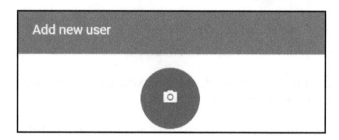

    2. Fill in the user information form. Assign a password for this account by doing one of the following:

    - Type a password:

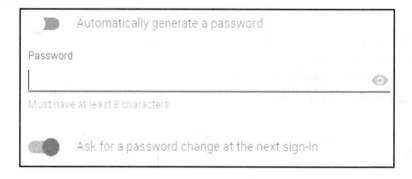

- Enable the option to automatically generate one:

3. Click **ADD NEW USER.**

- Click **Bulk upload users**: To create several users from a CSV file, just click **ATTACH CSV,** and choose the file where you store all of the new contacts information:

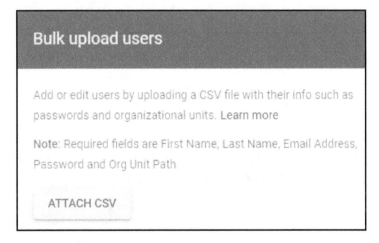

Click **UPLOAD.**

Bulk upload users is very convenient when dealing with large teams and, during migrations, you can download a template from the form or create a file using the following CSV structure:

```
First Name [Required],Last Name [Required],Email Address
[Required],Password [Required],Password Hash Function [UPLOAD ONLY],Org
Unit Path [Required],New Primary Email [UPLOAD ONLY],Home Secondary
Email,Work Secondary Email,Work Phone,Home Phone,Mobile Phone,Work
Address,Home Address,Employee ID,Employee Type,Employee Title,Manager
Email,Department,Cost Center,Building ID,Floor Name,Floor Section,Change
Password at Next Sign-In
```

You now know how to create new user accounts using the G Suite admin site; continue to the next section to learn how to add users using Google Domains instead.

Adding users with Google Domains

Google Domains allows you to quickly manage G Suite user accounts related to a particular domain, so you can easily add, remove, edit, or reset user passwords.

To add a new user, follow these steps from Google Domains:

1. Click **MANAGE** on the domain to which you wish to add a new user:

2. Click **Email** on the left-hand menu; the icon is shown in the following screenshot:

3. In the **Get a custom email address** section, follow these steps:
   1. Fill in the fields for first and last name of the new user
   2. Fill in the **Username** field; this will be the email address
   3. Select the role for this account:

   - Select **User** for accounts with no administrative privileges
   - Select **Admin** for accounts that can access G Suite for administrators for this domain

4. Click **ADD**.

5. Select the payment method or fill in the payment information:

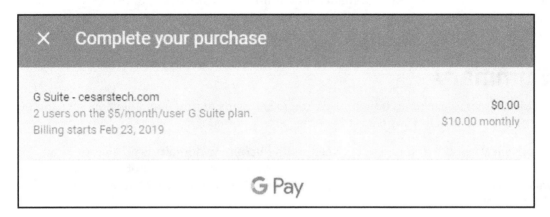

6. Click **BUY**.

You can also edit the accounts details or reset the password for an existing user from this view; to do so, find the account you wish to update and click **EDIT** on that row:

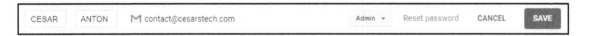

You can change a user's first and last names, as well as the role for that account; click **SAVE** to apply any changes.

Click on **Reset password** to send temporary login credentials to access this account; by default, the form will be automatically filled with that user's alternative address, but you can change it to any address the user requests. Click on **RESET PASSWORD** to send the credentials, as shown in the following screenshot:

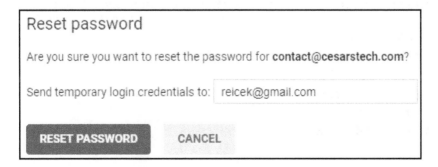

In this section, you learned how to switch between different domain administrator accounts, and how to add single users or in bulk. This will allow you to create accounts, as needed, no matter how many domains are within the organization, or even if you handle more than one organization.

Summary

In this chapter, we learned how to use Google Domains to find available domains and buy them, so you can help your team to get the perfect domain.

We also learned the differences between setting up a new domain as an alias or as an additional non-primary domain, as well as the differences between both approaches. With this, we can administer multiple domains for our clients and help them to manage their departments efficiently.

Getting a new domain is only the first step; we also learned how to create new user accounts, either one by one, or in bulk, and associate them to specific domains.

Now that we know how to manage multiple domains, we need to know how to monitor what's happening in our domains. In the next chapter, we will learn how to monitor all of the different reports that G Suite has to offer.

Further reading

- **Limitations with multiple domains** (https://support.google.com/a/answer/182081)
- **Best practices for accounts** (https://support.google.com/a/answer/1409688?hl=enref_topic=28609)
- **Add more domains to your G Suite or Cloud Identity account** (https://support.google.com/a/answer/7502379?visit_id=636837166547199177-2331447853rd=1)
- **Add a G Suite user** (https://support.google.com/domains/answer/6304542?hl=en)
- **Contact information** (https://support.google.com/domains/answer/3517907?hl=en#about)
- **Additional domains FAQ** (https://support.google.com/a/answer/175747?hl=en)

6
Monitoring Reports

Data-driven decisions can make a big difference in the competitiveness of a team. With this in mind, G Suite's business solutions include Reports that allows administrators to track almost everything that happens within the domain.

G Suite Reports are very powerful tools that concentrate years of careful thought and experience from Google, and are available to you as an administrator. The Reports feature was carefully designed and deeply integrated into G Suite services so you can always have accurate and updated information about your users.

Keep in mind that having access to detailed information only gets you so far. Imagine having a desk full of papers containing daily reports from the last five years and you need to compile the information there into a report that contains all the relevant information for your next meeting. Choosing the right metrics and charts to elaborate meaningful reports can be a complex task, where G Suite reports have you covered.

G Suite offers an extensive amount of reports that were designed to help you understand and keep track of things in a simple and intuitive way, so you can stay on top of everything.

In this chapter, you will learn how to do the following:

- Interpret **Highlights** reports
- Interpret security reports
- Interpret G Suite apps activity reports
- Interpret account activity reports
- Interpret and configure audit logs

Understanding Highlights reports

G Suite Highlights report allows you to take a quick glance at usage data for the different parts of G Suite, file sharing activities, the number of users in the domain, how much storage is being used, monitoring external app usage, and the number of users enrolled in 2-Step Verification.

Let's start by exploring the **USER STATUS** Highlights report.

Exploring USER STATUS Highlights

G Suite charges for each active account in the domain, so as an administrator, it's important for you to track the number of accounts in the domain as well as their individual statuses:

```
USER STATUS
Latest data available for: Jan 25, 2019

2
Users

● 0 Blocked

● 0 Suspended

● 0 Archived

● 2 Active
```

The G Suite **USER STATUS** Highlights report is on the top right of your screen, and it allows you to monitor the following:

- **Total number of users**: This is the total number of accounts in the domain.
- **Blocked**: The number of accounts that are currently blocked automatically by Google, usually because these accounts are reaching a quota limit (such as a certain amount of emails sent in a 24-hour period), or because of security concerns, such as the user being suspected of sending spam. Blocked accounts still have access to G Suite services, but are not able to send emails.

- **Suspended**: Users that have been temporarily blocked from accessing their accounts by an administrator. G Suite still charges for accounts that are suspended.
- **Archived**: These are the accounts that have been suspended and their information is stored in Google Vault. These accounts are billed as active accounts too.
- **Active**: This shows the number of accounts that are working without any restrictions.

You can also click on **USER STATUS** to open the **Account activity** report, which we will explore when we learn about User reports; for now, let's see what can we learn from the **SECURITY** Highlights report.

Exploring SECURITY Highlights

As an administrator, you can take a quick look at the **SECURITY** Highlights report to spot potential vulnerabilities by using the following security metrics:

- **External apps installed**: These are non-Google applications. As an administrator, it's important to keep an eye on these apps for potential security problems.
- **Users not enrolled in 2 Step Verification**: This is the number of users that are still not using the 2 Step Verification flow, which provides added security at the user level.
- **Users allowed access to less secure apps**: The number of users that have access to applications that do not have the highest possible security:

```
SECURITY
Latest data available for: Jan 24, 2019


1
External apps installed


2
Users not enrolled in 2 Step Verification


0
Users allowed access to less secure apps
```

You can also click on **SECURITY**, which functions as a shortcut for the **Users Security** report. In the next section, we will explore what we can learn in the **Apps usage activity highlights** report.

Exploring the Apps usage activity Highlights report

Here, you can easily monitor the usage of the different G Suite services in this domain during a specific period of time. This is very useful when you need to quickly check which services are in most demand by your team, so you can focus your attention where it's most needed:

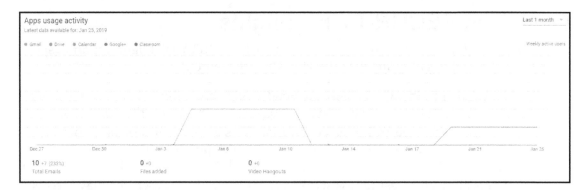

The usage activity Highlights report lets you monitor the following:

- **Gmail** web access
- **Drive** web access
- **Calendar** web access
- **Google+** web access
- **Classroom**, which is available in G Suite for Education
- **Total Emails** sent
- **Files added** to Drive
- Video Hangouts chats are not included in this count

You can filter the usage reports using the following time periods:

- **Last 7 days**
- **Last 1 month**
- **Last 3 months**
- **Last 6 months**

You now know how to check usage for different apps. Next, let's learn how to see how much data has been made accessible from outside the organization with the **File sharing activity** Highlights report.

Exploring the File sharing activity Highlights report

Sharing files is a basic requirement for collaboration, but doing it without caution can compromise your team's work.

Drive provides an easy and safe way for your users to share documents with other people, and one of the greatest advantages to a business using Drive is the ability to track how it is being used.

The **File sharing activity** report allows you to easily see how much is being shared in case there is some suspicious activity:

File sharing activity		Last 7 days ▼
Latest data available for: Jan 25, 2019		

↑0
External shares

Public	—0
Anyone With Link	—0
Outside Domain	—0

↑0
Internal shares

Anyone In Domain	—0
Anyone In Domain With Link	—0
Within Domain	—0
Private	—0

The report classifies sharing as follows:

- **External shares**: These are files shared to people outside of the organization and it's important to pay attention to these numbers to avoid unwanted information leaks. These sharing numbers are classified using the following statuses:
    - **Public**: These are available to anyone and might appear in Google search results, even for people outside the organization, and can be accessed even without a Google account
    - **Anyone With Link**: These are available for anyone that has the sharing URL
    - **Outside Domain**: These are shared directly with a Google account that is not part of the domain
- **Internal shares**: These are files shared within the organization. These sharing numbers are classified using the following statuses:
    - **Anyone In Domain**: Any member of the domain can see and find them
    - **Anyone In Domain With Link**: Anyone in the domain that has the URL can see them
    - **Within Domain**: Files that were shared with a specific member or members of a team
    - **Private**: Files that can only be seen by the owner

Now that we've explored options that allow us to quickly check app usage details in G Suite, let's learn how to get more detailed usage information in the next section.

Understanding Apps reports

G Suite comes with many productivity applications to facilitate your team's work every day. As an administrator, you can keep track of how much each part of G Suite is being used so that you can prioritize the administration of the most-used parts, as well as help your users understand how they can make the most out of the least-used services.

Accounts

Administering accounts is a big part of your duties as an administrator. This is particularly important in large teams since the amount billed every month depends on the amount of user accounts.

You can see the following reports in this section:

- **2-Step verification enrollment**: The number of users that have already enrolled in the 2-Step verification flow in the selected period:

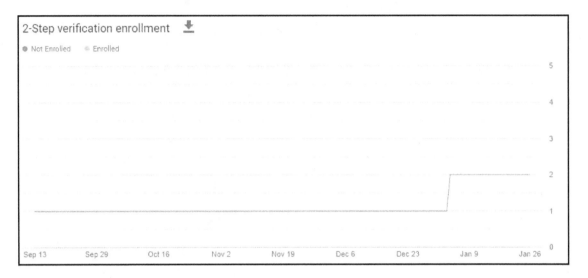

- **2-Step verification enforcement**: The number of users that were required to use 2-Step verification to log in, and their different statuses:

These statuses, as shown in the previous graphs, are as follows:

- **Locked**: The number of users that are required to use 2-step verification, and right now, are not allowed into the system for not complying on time.
- **Not Enrolled**: The number of users that have not joined the 2-step verification flow.

- **Not Enforced**: The number of users that have not been required to join the 2-step verification flow. These users will never be locked, even if they don't use 2-step verification.
- **Enrolled**: The number of users that have enabled the 2-step verification flow.
- **Enforced**: The number of users that are required to use the 2-step verification flow.

- **User account status**: This shows the number of user accounts on each status during the selected period:

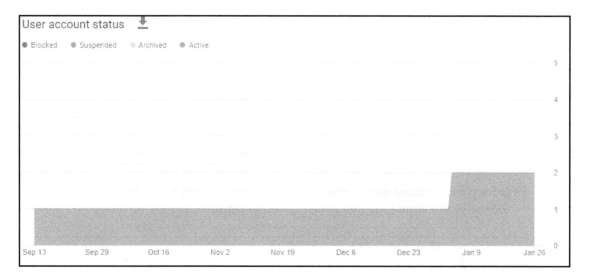

You may have noticed an icon next to the report's name; let's see what it does in the next section.

Downloading a report

If you click on the download icon next to the name of a report, you will see the following options:

- **Export to Google Sheets**: This will automatically generate a Google spreadsheet pre-filled with the raw information used to generate this report. You can use this exported spreadsheet to generate a custom report, to see all the information in detail, or to keep it as a record:

- **Download as CSV file**: Similar to exporting to a spreadsheet, but this will download a CSV file instead. This files makes it easier to export data that can be ingested by external software, but be careful, since this is a copy of potentially sensitive information, and it cannot be tracked like a spreadsheet.

Now that we know what we can learn from the accounts report, let's continue and learn about **App Maker** reports in the next section.

App Maker

App Maker is an awesome tool that allows members of your organization to create powerful applications with little or no coding. These reports will allow you to monitor the general usage of App Maker by members of the organization, as well as each one of the projects that have been created. We will be learning how to use Google App Maker in Chapter 9, *Creating Sites and Getting Started with App Maker*.

You can see the following reports in this section:

- **Users**: Here you can see how many active users it had in a time period:

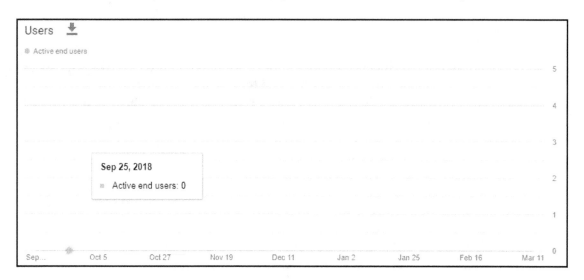

- **Projects**: Here you will see a list of the projects within this domain and how many users worked on those projects in a time period:

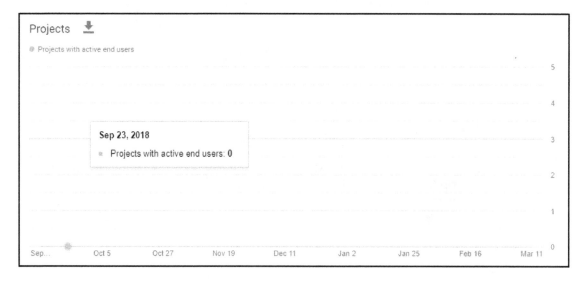

We just learned how to track the use of Google App Maker within our organization. Let's continue with **Classroom** reports.

Classroom

Google Classroom is a special tool for educational organizations, such as schools, that helps them go paperless on assignments, as well as improve communication and collaboration.

In this section, you can see the following reports:

- **Active classes**: This is a timeline of the number of active classes:

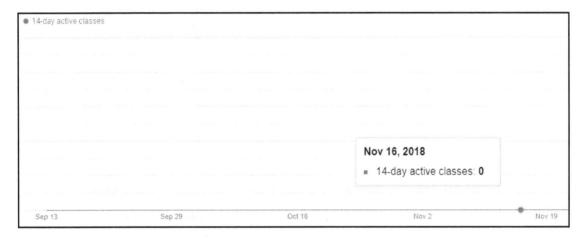

- **Classes created**: This is a timeline of the classes that have been created
- **Posts created**: This is a timeline of the number of posts created by teachers and students

We have learned what we can see from the **Classroom** reports, so to continue in the order of the menu, let's learn about the **Cloud Search** report.

Cloud Search

Google Cloud Search allows your users to search for specific information anywhere within the domain, using the technology that Google uses to power its search engine:

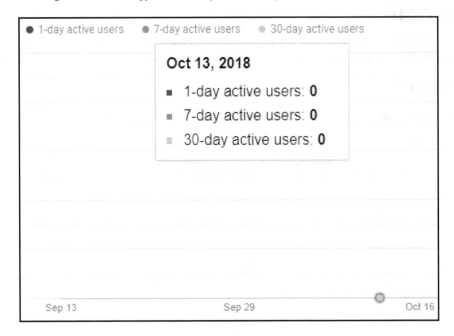

In the **Cloud Search** report, you can see a timeline for the following metrics:

- **1-day active users**: Gives you the number of Cloud Search users for that day
- **7-day active users**: The number of Cloud Search users in the previous 7 days
- **30-day active users**: The number of users that had used Cloud Search in the previous 30 days

Now that you know how to track Cloud Search usage within a domain, let's see what the **Drive** report has for us.

Drive

Google Drive is a very important tool that allows safe and efficient collaboration within our teams, but to keep things safe, it's important to keep an eye on how much our users are sharing.

In this section, you can see the following reports:

- **External shares**: This is very important, since it lets you know how often users are sharing things outside the organization. Always keep an eye on days or periods with unusual increases:

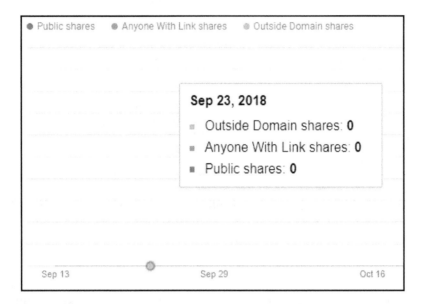

- **Internal shares**: This shows us how much our users are sharing internally:

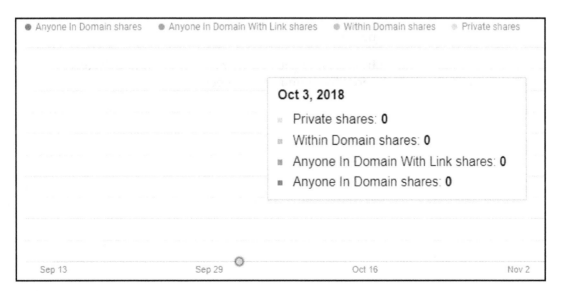

- **Files added**: This is the count of each kind of file that was created in the organization for you to have a very detailed view of what kind of content users are creating:

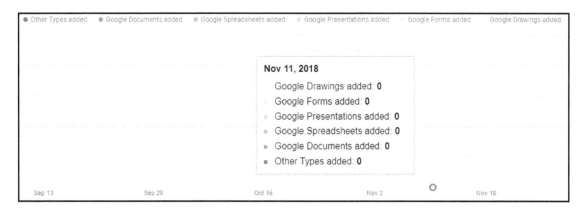

This concludes our overview of the Drive usage report. Let's explore **Gmail** usage in the next section.

Gmail

Gmail is a very important part of business communication, and this report will show you how many emails are going through the domain and also analyze the kinds of messages that are being sent.

This section shows the following reports:

- **Inbound Email: Delivery**: Here you can see how the amount of **Rejected, Rerouted**, and **Delivered** inbound messages per day:

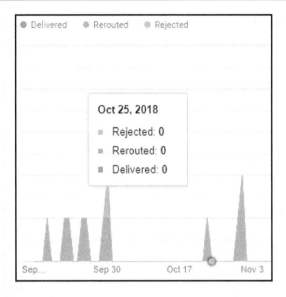

- **Inbound Email: Spam**: Here you can see the comparison between **Spam** and **Not Spam** inbound messages received:

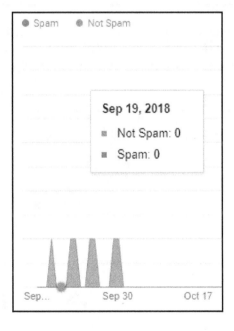

- **Inbound Email: Encryption**: This will show you the inbound **Encrypted** versus **Not Encrypted** messages:

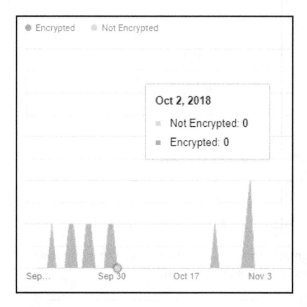

- **Outbound Email: Delivery**: In this chart, you can easily compare the amount of outbound **Rejected**, **Rerouted**, and **Delivered** messages. Pay special attention to the **Rejected** messages, as some users may need help communicating with another domain:

- **Outbound Email: Encryption**: This timeline shows you the amount of **Encrypted** versus **Not Encrypted** messages that were sent from this domain:

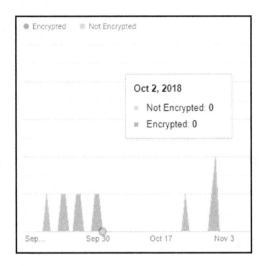

- **Total emails**: This shows the total emails sent and received in this domain:

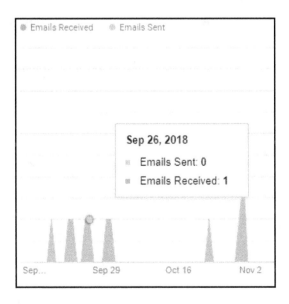

As you can see, using reports to get an overview of Gmail-related activity is very easy, and will make it easier for you to spot unusual activity. Let's continue our journey through G Suite **Apps** reports by exploring the different metrics of Google+ in the next section.

Google+

In June 2011, Google launched its own social media platform called Google+. Although it failed to effectively compete with other platforms such as Facebook, it had good acceptance with professionals and businesses by proving an effective tool to build dedicated communities.

In October 2018, Google announced that it will sunset the consumer version of Google+ and focus only on the business version. This will allow the platform to focus on features that businesses need; from giving admins more control over Google+, to more detailed reports.

With Google+ for Business, you can create a dedicated social network for your domain, either for internal use, or to build a community around a business or product.

In this section, we will learn about the different reports for Google+ and their metrics.

Aggregate Reports

Aggregate Reports for Google+ provide a convenient set of charts that will help you analyze various trends in your communities:

- **Active Users**: This will give you a timeline of users with filters for **1-Day**, **7-Day**, and **30-Day** user activity:

- **New Users**: Here you can see a timeline of the new users in Google+ for your domain.
- **Communities**: This is a timeline with the following metrics:

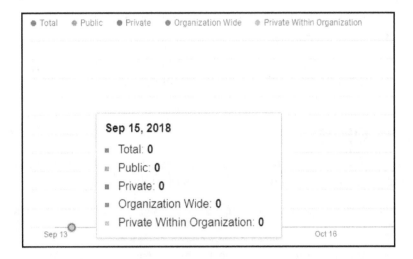

- **Total**: This is the total number of communities for this domain
- **Public**: Anyone can join, even outside the organization
- **Private**: Members can only join by invitation
- **Organization Wide**: Anyone in the organization can join
- **Private Within Organization**: Only invited members of your organization can join

- **Collections**: This is a timeline with the total number of collections that were registered each day.
- **New Posts**: This is a timeline with the number of new posts that were published each day. This tells you how many new topics are being generated.
- **New Comments**: This is a timeline with the total number of new comments posted each day. With this, you can see how much your users are engaging in conversations. It's a good practice to strike a balance between new posts and comments in your communities.
- **New +1s**: A timeline with the number of +1s that users used each day. High numbers usually mean something interesting happened.
- **Posts Viewed**: This timeline shows how many views the posts are getting; ideally, this number should keep a relatively steady rate of growth.

- **Posts Reshared**: This timeline will tell you how many posts are being reshared. It's a good idea to keep an eye on the balance between posts viewed, reshared, and those that got a +1, since this will tell you how much interest the users are showing.
- **Video Hangouts**: In this timeline, you can keep track of how many video Hangouts meetings happened per day.

With these reports, you can keep track of your social networks and easily spot trends so you can identify what makes your team and your clients excited.

Hangouts Chat

Hangouts Chat offers a robust real-time chat platform where users can write directly to each other, or create rooms to gather several users in a single chat.

Let's explore the different reports and their metrics so we can easily keep track of user's activity:

- **Created Rooms**: Here you can see a timeline that shows the number of chats grouped in three types. This gives you a quick idea of how many users are creating rooms and how often:

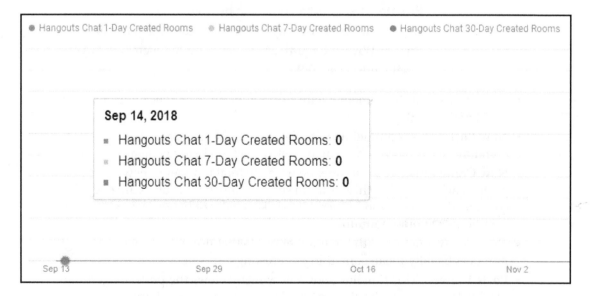

- **Hangouts Chat 1-Day**: These chats had activity on a particular date
- **Hangouts Chat 7-Day**: These are chats that were active within seven days of a particular date
- **Hangouts Chat 30-Day**: These are chats that were active within 30 days of a particular date

- **Active Rooms**: This timeline will let you see much users were talking to each other on a particular date. It's usually recommended to remove rooms within the 30-day range:

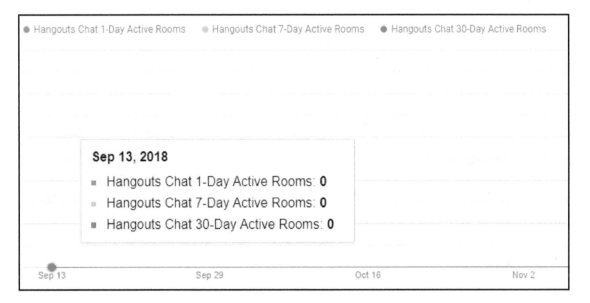

- **Active Users**: This shows whether the users are actively using chats:

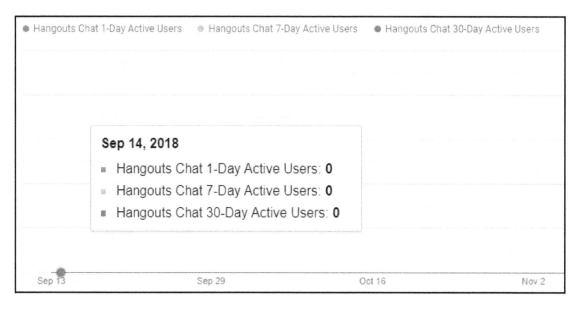

- **Messages Posted**: This will show you how many messages were posted on a particular date. All 1-Day messages will eventually become 30-Day ones; these numbers will let you see spikes and drops of user engagement through chats:

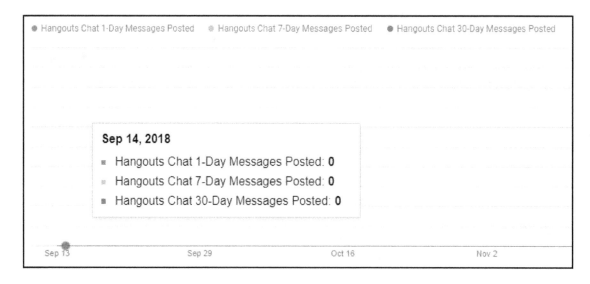

Hangouts Chat reports will make it easier to spot the most and least active users and rooms in this domain.

We now know how to explore the **Apps** reports, and track the use of the different parts of G Suite so we can focus only on what we need to.

Let's continue to the next section to learn what kind of mobile devices are being used to access G Suite.

Understanding the Mobile Devices report

G Suite not only works great on mobile devices, but it also allows administrators to keep detailed track of the kind of devices being used by members of the organization thanks to eight different reports.

To simplify things, all reports comes can be analyzed in two aggregations:

- **7DA**: These are reports that show activity over seven days
- **30DA**: These are reports that show activity over 30 days

G Suite divides Mobile Devices reports into four categories:

- **Managed Devices**: Here you can track access using any managed device.
- **Managed Users**: This keeps track of users who sync their accounts to a mobile device:

- **Managed Android Devices**: Here you can track the number of Android devices grouped by Android version. This allows you to keep track of the popularity of each Android version in the organization.
- **Managed iOS Devices**: Here you can track the number of iOS devices grouped by iOS version so you can keep track of what the most-used iOS versions in the organization are:

Keeping track of devices and versions also allows you to track cases of users using very old versions that might be missing new features.

Understanding the Users report

The **Users** report gives administrators the ability to focus on a particular user or a particular activity, as well as to compare users by selecting different metrics and filters.

Above the account activity report, you will see a dynamic timeline that shows your users' activity through time; this can give you many insights into your team's activities. Click on the name of the metric to see a list with all the available options:

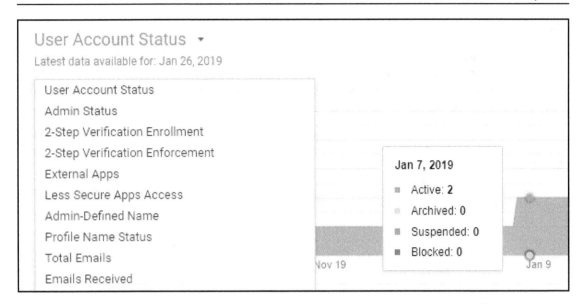

Below the timeline, you will see a dynamic table with aggregate information that will allow you to easily compare your users:

If you click on a column name, the chart will show the timeline for that metric, and you can select the columns on display by clicking on the **Select columns** ⣿ icon (the icon that looks like three gray lines) and choosing the metrics you are looking for.

Since there are so many metrics that you can select, G Suite has selected the three that are usually the most used so you can quickly go to those reports; once there, you can change the active timeline or the visible columns as you see fit.

These are the default activity reports:

- **Account activity**: This will show you a table with **User Account Status**, **Admin Status**, and **2-Step Verification Enrollment** as the default columns. On top you can see a timeline that shows the **User Account Status** evolution, click on the title to change the metric to **Admin Status**, or **2-Step Verification Enrollment**:

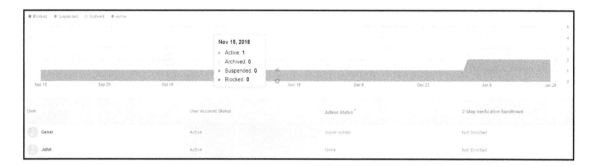

- **Apps usage activity**: This will show you the **Total Storage Used** timeline, a table with **Total Storage Used**, **Total Emails**, **Files added**, and **Search Queries** as the default columns:

- **Security**: This will show you the **External Apps** timeline and a table with **External Apps**, **2-Step Verification Enrollment**, **External shares**, and **Internal shares** as the default columns:

Being able to understand user reports will help you stay on top of almost any relevant aspect of their activity within the domain, which can be extremely useful for human resources when it comes to finding what makes your team more productive, focusing administrative efforts, and helping prevent security problems. These are just some of the many ways you and your team can take advantage of G Suite user reports.

Reports are a great tool for analysis, but we might need more specific information when we need to dig deeper, so let's explore audit logs in the next section.

Understanding audit logs

Audit logs keep detailed records of key events in the system, and are designed so you can easily find what you are looking for when you need to know all the details about an event or series of events.

All logs are classified in 14 different categories, and each one keeps different parameters about the events it stores. By default, all logs will be showing the parameters that are considered most commonly used, but you can customize to show additional parameters when available and hide the ones you might not be interested in at that moment.

The email log search is the only one that has no selectable columns, but instead has several search fields to make it easier to find exactly what you need.

Let's explore what each of these categories can show us, as well as which column each one has enabled by default, and which ones we need to enable if we need to:

- **Admin**: This shows a record of all actions performed by the administrators of the domain:

- **Login**: Here you can track each user login, including the IP address they logged, which is very useful for tracking locations, spotting suspicious logins, or accessing from unauthorized locations:

- **SAML**: Use this to track login and logout attempts to and from applications that use the **Security Assertion Markup Language (SAML)**:

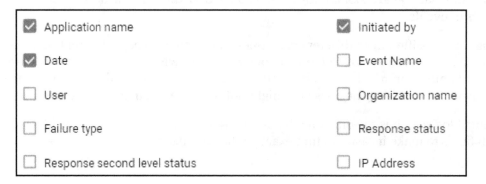

- **LDAP**: The **Lightweight Directory Access Protocol (LDAP)** log will show you details related to applications that use that protocol to integrate with **Cloud Identity** or G Suite:

☑ Event Name	☑ Application Name
☐ Application Id	☐ User
☑ Date	☐ IP Address
☐ Attributes	☐ Deref Aliases
☐ Base Object	☐ Connection Id
☐ Filter	☐ Is Types Only
☐ Result Code	☐ Message ID
☐ Name	☐ Request Controls
☐ Result Controls	☐ Scope
☐ Size Limit	☐ Time Limit
☐ Version	

- **Drive**: This will keep track of all actions performed using Google Drive within the domain. For example, you can use this to track the history of a file:

☑ Event Description	☐ User
☑ Date	☐ Event Name
☐ Item Id	☐ Item Type
☐ Owner	☐ Prior Visibility
☐ Visibility	☐ IP Address

- **Calendar**: This will keep track of all calendar events, errors, and operations that involved G Suite Calendar in this domain:

☑ User	☐ Calendar Id
☐ Event Title	☐ Event Id
☐ API Kind	☐ User Agent
☐ Recipient Email	☐ Message Id
☐ Remote EWS URL	☐ Error Code
☐ Requested Window Start	☐ Requested Window End
☐ Date	☐ IP Address

- **Devices**: This will keep a log of activities performed on computers and mobile devices connected to your domain:

☐ Event Name	☐ User
☐ Device Type	☐ Application hash

- **Token**: With OAuth token logs, you can keep track of the domains users' access to third-party applications:

☐ Event Name	☐ User
☐ Application Name	☐ Client Id
☐ Scope	☐ IP Address
☑ Date	

- **Groups**: Use this when you need to track changes, memberships, and messages for groups in this domain:

- **Hangouts Chat**: Used to track Hangouts Chat activity with members of the organization:

- **Google+**: Use this to track how members of the organization are using Google+:

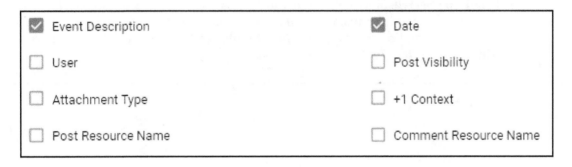

- **Hangouts Meet**: This log keeps detailed information about the video conferences performed in the organization:

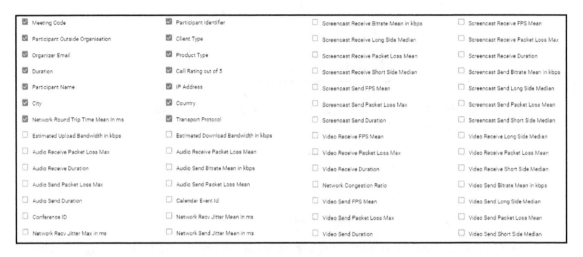

- **Email Log Search**: Since email logs can be very extensive, for this log, instead of having selectable columns, we have a searching tool specifically designed to find emails. You can find messages by **Date**, **Sender** address, **Sender IP**, **Recipient** address, **Recipient IP**, **Subject**, or **Message ID**:

Being able to access the audit logs will prove very useful when you have an alert and need to find details about that or any other event.

Now that you know how to track events using the audit logs, let's make sure you become aware of them as fast as possible by learning how to manage alerts within G Suite in the next section.

Managing alerts

Reports are an amazing tool for identifying trends, and searching logs allows you to trace specific events, but they both depend on you spending time finding relevant information.

G Suite Alerts provide email notifications when certain events take place. As an administrator, you can choose for which events you wish to be notified immediately.

The alert screen has three columns:

- **Alert name**: This is a short description of the event.
- **Email recipients**: Which group will be notified of this event.
- **Status**: Indicates whether the event is enabled or disabled. To change the status of an event, just click on the toggle slider:

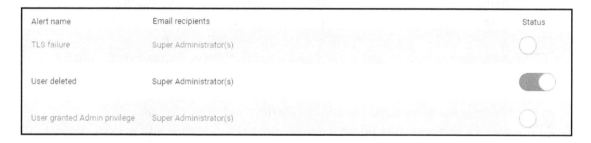

At the moment of writing this, there are 21 different alerts to choose from. Let's explore them so you can choose which ones you need on your domains:

- **Drive settings changed**: Sends a message when an administrator changes the default Drive settings for this domain.
- **TLS failure**: This will inform you when messages marked as required to use TLS could not be delivered or received.
- **User deleted**: Sends a message when an account was deleted from the system.
- **User granted Admin privilege**: Triggers when some user has been granted administrative privileges.
- **Exchange journaling failure**: This notifications trigger when Google Vault is having problems connecting to Microsoft Exchange servers.
- **Suspended user made active**: Sends a notification when a suspended account becomes activated.
- **User's Admin privilege revoked**: Sends a notification when an account is changed from administrator to regular.

- **Smarthost failure**: This will notify you if an usual amount of messages fail to be delivered to one of your smart hosts. You can use the IP in the notification to find more details in the email log.
- **Email settings changed**: This notifies you when an administrator changes the Gmail defaults for this domain.
- **User's password changed**: With this alert enabled, administrators will be notified when any account gets a new password within the domain. This can help you keep track of whether users are updating their password.
- **User suspended**: This notification is sent when an administrator suspends an account.
- **Suspicious login activity**: With this notification, administrators will be notified when there is suspicious login activity on one of the accounts.
- **Calendar settings changed**: This will send a notification when an administrator changes the default configuration for Google Calendar on this domain.
- **Apps outage alert**: If there is a problem with Google servers, this alert will notify the administrators. I recommend enabling this just in case.
- **New user added**: This alert will send a notification every time an account is created.
- **Mobile settings changed**: A notification will be sent when an administrator changes the default settings for mobile devices in this domain.
- **Device compromise update**: This will send you a notification when a device that has access to this domain is compromised or mark it as no longer compromised. You can see more details in the **Devices** log.
- **Suspicious mobile activity**: When this alert enabled, administrators will be notified of suspicious activity in any of the devices that have access to the domain.
- **Rate limited recipient**: This alert gets triggered when there is a suspiciously large amount of inbound emails in the domain, which could be caused by a malicious attack.
- **Government-backed attack warning**: This is a special kind of notification that the Google team sends you when they suspect that your domain has received government-backed attacks attempting to compromise some account. This warning will include personalized guidance with steps to take to protect the domain.
- **Google operations**: This is another special alert that you will receive when Google suspects there is a potential security or privacy issue that is affecting G Suite services for your domain.

Summary

Congratulations for finishing this chapter! You have just learned how to monitor an entire domain, regardless of how many users it may have.

You are now capable of quickly analyzing how your users interact with G Suite; you can measure the popularity of a service, or the productivity of a team or individual with the **Apps usage activity** Highlights report.

Sharing is a basic need for collaboration, and with the **File sharing activity** Highlights report, you can keep track of how information is moving and track down any suspicious activity using the **Audit** logs.

We learned how to track the way users are using all the different G Suite main components thanks to the many **Apps** reports; you can see all relevant activity through dynamic reports with the most relevant metrics about Accounts, App Maker, Classroom, Cloud Search, Drive, Gmail, Google+, and Hangouts.

Sometimes you want to know how your users are accessing their accounts, and for that, we learned how to understand the **Mobile Devices** report and how it can quickly show what devices are being used, and even the versions of the systems.

As a team grows, the task of managing users becomes increasingly important, and in this chapter, we learned how to understand the different users reports, so you can keep track of who has complied with security and how active your users are.

We learned about all the different reports in G Suite, but sometimes, you need detailed information about a particular event or series of events, and for that, we learned how to use the different audit logs.

We closed this chapter by learning how to manage alerts so that we are always notified immediately about events that might require quick action.

Now that you know how to use reports, logs, and alerts, it's time to continue to the next chapter and learn how to find anything that has been said or done in the domain with **Vault** and **eDiscovery**.

Further reading

- **Alert center for G Suite generally available to help identify security threats** (`https://gsuiteupdates.googleblog.com/2018/10/g-suite-alert-center-generally-available.html`), *G Suite Updates*, October 10, 2018
- **Monitor usage and security with reports** (`https://support.google.com/a/answer/6000239?hl=enref_topic=6046029`)
- **Understanding audit logs** (`https://support.google.com/a/topic/9027054`)

7
Archiving with Vault

Organizations nowadays are well aware of the need for keeping detailed reports. This is not only useful for the organization—it is also a compliance mandate. However, being able to capture and store all information that conforms to compliance requirements is challenging for organizations lacking the necessary tools and experience.

This chapter will discuss Google Vault, which is a tool that was designed to assist organizations with legal requirements pertaining to information retention. Vault is particularly useful while facing legal inquiries, performing investigations, and responding to a request for records.

Google Vault is included with no extra cost in G Suite for Business, but can also be bought separately with a monthly fee. In this chapter, you will learn how to use the power of Vault and eDiscovery to find virtually anything that was ever done, or happened within the organization's G Suite.

After reading this chapter, you will have learned how to do the following:

- Set up retention rules
- Create matters
- Use eDiscovery to search through the organization's data, as well as complete the following steps:
    - Saving the query
    - Exporting the results
- Use audit to export Vaults logs

To access Vault, open a new browser tab and go to `https://ediscovery.google.com/discovery/`.

If you are using a personal account on the same browser, you might have trouble accessing Vault. To fix this, open Vault in incognito mode.

Setting up Retention

In this section, we will have a look at retention rules and how they can be used to sort information that needs to be preserved. Defining retention rules is the first step toward setting up Vault. Retention rules are a set of instructions that direct Vault on what files to keep, and for how long.

There are two types of retention rules, as follows:

- **Custom retention rules**: These rules allows you to specify the retention period for data that meets specific criteria.
- **Default retention rules**: With these, you can define rules that apply to the entire organization. These are only applied when there is no applicable custom rule or legal hold.

To set up retention rules, click **Retention** on Vault's left menu, as shown in the following screenshot:

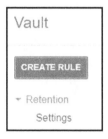

 It is important to be very careful when defining or changing retention rules since it may cause permanent loss of data in the domain.

Defining default retention rules

Default retention rules define the general retention guidelines for Vault to apply over the different G Suite components. Keep in mind that Vault will apply these rules, unless told otherwise, by a custom retention rule or a hold, which we will explore later in this chapter.

Let's start defining our defaults by setting up Gmail retention rules in the next section.

Defining Mail default retention rules

Email messages are a very common source for security problems, so keeping an adequate record can be very helpful when investigating an incident.

Follow these steps to set the default retention rules for all email messages:

1. Click on the **Mail** tab.
2. Enable **Set a default retention rule for Mail**.
3. Set the **Duration** to one of the following options:
    *   **Indefinitely**: This will keep the messages for as long as the account exists. I recommend using this option.
    *   N **days from when the message was sent**: This will keep the messages for the amount of days set here. You can specify a period of up to 36500 days (100 years). If you set a limit, then you must also set the **Action after expiration**, as follows:
        *   **Expunge deleted messages**: This will erase the messages that the user has already deleted
        *   **Expunge all messages**: This will erase all messages that are older than the retention period
4. Click **Save.**
5. If you set a retention limit, you will be asked to confirm that you understand the consequences. Please read and confirm each.

Now that we have set the retention rules for email messages, let's set up retention rules for Drive in the next section.

Defining Drive default retention rules

Drive allows users to create, store, and share files and documents without the need for physical storage. Another advantage of using Drive is that all files will be subject to Vault retention rules, and all the information can be located using eDiscovery.

Setting up retention rules for Drive allows you to define for how long the system should keep a copy of files, even after the user has deleted them.

The following steps demonstrate how to set up Drive default retention rules:

1. Click on the **Drive** tab.
2. Enable **Set a default retention rule for Drive**.
3. Set the **Duration** to one of the following options:
   - **Indefinitely**: This will keep the messages for as long as the account exists. I recommend using this option.
   - N **days from when the file was created or last modified**: This will keep the messages for the amount of days set here. You can specify a period of up to 36500 days (100 years). If you set a limit, then you must also set the **Action after expiration**, as follows:
     - **Expunge deleted files**: This will erase the messages that the user has already deleted
     - **Expunge all files**: This will erase all messages that are older than the retention period

4. Click **Save**.
5. If you set a retention limit, you will be asked to confirm that you understand the consequences. Please read and confirm each.

We now have emails and files covered. In the next section, you will learn how to set up retention rules for group messages.

Defining Groups default retention rules

Previously, we learned how Groups allow administrators to create special emails that allow you to create custom email addresses that handle specific topics, and users can subscribe to them to facilitate routing messages. A very common example for a support group would be support@yourdomain.com.

Keeping a copy of these messages is important, so let's see how we can set up retention rules so that we can define for how long the system should keep them.

Follow these steps to configure Groups default retention rules:

1. Click on the **Groups** tab.
2. Enable **Set a default retention rule for Groups**.

3. Set the **Duration** to one of the following options:
   - **Indefinitely**: This will keep the messages for as long as the account exists. I recommend using this option.
   - N **days from when the message was sent**: This will keep the messages for the amount of days set here. You can specify a period of up to 36500 days (100 years). If you set a limit, then you must also set the **Action after expiration**, as follows:
     - **Expunge deleted messages**: This will erase the messages that the user has already deleted
     - **Expunge all messages**: This will erase all messages that are older than the retention period

4. Click **Save**.
5. If you set a retention limit, you will be asked to confirm that you understand the consequences. Please read and confirm each.

Now that you have mails, files, and groups covered, let's continue by setting up the Hangouts Chat log retention rules in the next section.

Defining Hangouts Chat default retention rules

Chats are a great tool that allow users in the domain to communicate with text messages much faster than using emails.

Keeping a log of that communication can be extremely useful when some important piece of information was mentioned in a chat, but no one took note, or when there was a security problem and you need to investigate all related communications.

Let's start by setting the default retention rules for all Hangouts Chat messages by following these steps:

1. Click on the **Hangouts Chat** tab.
2. Enable **Set a default retention rule for Hangouts Chat**.
3. Set the **Duration** to one of the following options:
   - **Indefinitely**: This will keep the messages for as long as the account exists. I recommend using this option.

- N **days from when the message was sent**: This will keep the messages for the amount of days set here. You can specify a period of up to 36500 days (100 years). If you set a limit, then you must also set the **Action after expiration**, as follows:
    - **Expunge deleted messages**: This will erase the messages that the user has already deleted
    - **Expunge all messages**: This will erase all messages that are older than the retention period

4. Click **Save**.
5. If you set a retention limit, you will be asked to confirm that you understand the consequences. Please read and confirm each.

Now that you know how to define Hangouts Chat retention rules so that you can save the day next time, there's a need to find something that was said in a chat. In the next section, we will learn how to do this for Hangouts Meet.

Defining Hangouts Meet default retention rules

Hangouts Meet offers a video conference solution that is easy to use, highly reliable, and offers advanced functionalities. It also offers integration with Calendar, so that it can be the location or an alternative for a meeting, and Drive, so that users can share files and collaborate on documents in real time.

Important things are usually said during recorded meetings, and administrators can keep a record of this meeting so that users can review it later. Keep in mind that users must manually start the recording of a meeting.

To configure retention rules for Hangouts Meet, follow these steps:

1. Click on the **Hangouts Meet** tab.
2. Enable **Set a default retention rule for Hangouts Meet**.
3. Set the **Duration** to one of the following options:
    - **Indefinitely**: This will keep the messages for as long as the account exists. I recommend using this option.

- N **days from when the file was created or last modified**: This will keep the messages for the amount of days set here. You can specify a period of up to 36500 days (100 years). If you set a limit, then you must also set the **Action after expiration**, as follows:
    - **Expunge deleted files**: This will erase the messages that the user has already deleted
    - **Expunge all files**: This will erase all messages that are older than the retention period

4. Click **Save**.
5. If you set a retention limit, you will be asked to confirm that you understand the consequences. Please read and confirm each.

Congratulations—you have just finished setting up all the default retention rules. Now, your company is better protected against legal problems related to information within G Suite.

In some cases, you might need to set up custom retention rules that apply to special conditions. In the next section, you will learn how to set them up.

Creating custom retention rules

Depending on the nature of the organization, G Suite administrators might need to pay particular attention to messages or documents that match some specific criteria. Custom retention rules allow administrators to define retention rules that apply to specific scenarios, such as a specific word or phrase on a file, chat, or email.

Use custom rules to target special cases where there might be a legal issue that won't fall under the general retention rule, or to set them apart from the rest of the information to facilitate the investigation of a matter.

For retention rules, it's usually best to be as broad as possible. This way, we can be sure that the necessary information will be available:

1. To set up custom retention rules, click on **Retention** on Vault's left menu and then click the **CREATE RULE** button:

2. This will take you to a form where you must select where the new rule will apply, as shown in the following screenshot:

Vault allows custom retention rules for **Mail**, **Drive**, **Groups**, **Hangouts Chat**, and **Hangouts Meet**. In the following sections, we will explore how to set up your new rule, depending on which component it will target.

Continue reading to explore how to set up each kind of custom rule.

Defining Mail retention rules

A custom email retention rule allows you to catch emails that happened within a time period, or that has content that matches a specific criteria.

Use a combination of these filters to target scenarios that could lead to potential legal issues, like the word `confidential`, or something that happened within the time frame where we know there was an issue.

To create a custom email retention rule, follow these steps:

1. Select the organizational unit you wish to target:

2. Define the conditions for the messages you wish to target. These could be any of the following:
   - From which **Sent date**.
   - To which **Sent date.**
   - **Terms** defined by search operators. The following screenshot shows these options:

3. Set the duration for this rule; I recommend using **Indefinitely** and change it later, but only if necessary. This is the number of days that the system will wait before taking action after a message is sent:

Define the **Action after expiration** if you chose a specific number days:

- **Expunge just the messages that users have already deleted** will only remove messages that have been there more than the days defined by this rule and that have also been deleted by the user. This is recommended to avoid unwanted data loss.
- **Expunge all messages** will remove everything that is older than the specified days. This can be frustrating for users and might lead to unwanted data loss.

4. Click **SAVE**.

Now, your new rule will be available in the **Custom retention rules** table. Here, you can also review all current custom rules main settings, as shown in the following screenshot:

Creating custom retention rules will help you prepare for legal issues over these kind of messages. In the next section, you will learn how to define custom Drive retention rules.

Defining Drive retention rules

One big advantage of using Google Drive within an organization is the ability to track everything that happens to a file. You can create a retention rule to target potential legal issues like a team that works with prototypes, an entire organization, or a user that has sensitive information, and so on.

To add a custom Drive retention rule, follow these steps:

1. Define the **Entity** you wish to apply the rule to, as follows:

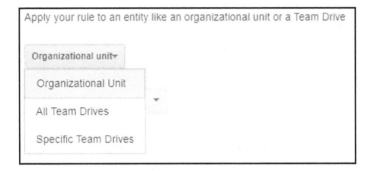

- Select **Organizational Unit** to target all members of a domain, or an organization unit within it
- Select **All Team Drives** to keep files that are shared across entire teams
- Select **Specific Team Drives** to target only a team with particular specifics by following these steps:

1. Click **Find Team Drives**, as shown here:

2. Write the name of a user that belongs to the Team Drive you wish to target. The system provides a quick search feature to make this easier:

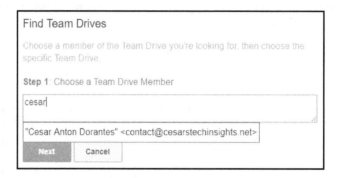

3. Click **Next**.

4. Write the name of the Team Drive you are going to target. The system also provides an autocomplete feature to facilitate finding the name:

5. Click **Done** to add the Team Drive as the target for this rule:

2. Set the **Duration** for this rule; I recommend using **Indefinitely** and changing it later, but only if necessary. This is the number of days that the system will wait before taking action after a file is **Created**, **Last modified**, or **Moved to trash**:

Define the **Action after expiration** if you choose a specific number of days, as follows:

- **Expunge just the files that users have already deleted** will only remove files that have been there more than the days defined by this rule and that have also been deleted by the user. This is recommended to avoid unwanted data loss.
- **Expunge all files** will remove everything that is older than the specified days. Avoid when possible, since it can be frustrating for users, and might lead to unwanted data loss.

3. Click **SAVE**.

You can confirm the settings of your new rule by taking a look at the **Custom retention rules** table, as shown in the following screenshot:

By carefully setting up Drive custom retention rules, you can be sure the system will keep the information that's required to deal with legal issues related to files. Let's continue to the next section to learn how to create Groups retention rules.

Defining Groups retention rules

Groups messages can be particularly important to keep for legal issues, especially those related to sensitive information, or those that route important messages.

It's a good idea to set custom retention rules for external communication groups like `contact`, `support`, and `sales`, or anything that may contain useful information if there is a related legal situation.

To define a new Group retention rule, follow these steps:

1. Define the kind of groups this rule will target:

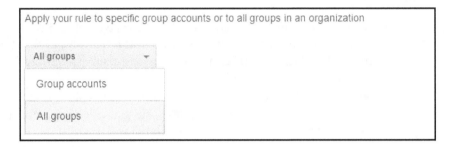

- Select **Group accounts** to target specific groups:
    - Write the name of the groups you wish to target; Vault provides an autocomplete feature to facilitate finding the name.
- Select **All Groups** if you wish the rule to apply to every group.
- Define the **Conditions** for the messages you wish to target. These could be any of the following:
    - From which **Sent date.**
    - To which **Sent date.**
    - **Terms** defined by search operators. The following screenshot shows these options:

2. Set the **Duration** for this rule; I recommend using **Indefinitely** and changing it later, but only if necessary. This is the number of days that the system will wait before taking action after a message is sent:

Define the **Action after expiration** if you chose a specific number days, as follows:

- **Expunge just the messages that users have already deleted** will only remove messages that have been there more than the days defined by this rule and that have also been deleted by the user. This is recommended to avoid unwanted data loss.
- **Expunge all messages** will remove everything that is older than the specified days. This can be frustrating for users, and might lead to unwanted data loss.

3. Click **SAVE**.

Remember to validate that your rule was created properly by taking a look at the **Custom retention rules** table.

Now that you know how to define Groups custom retention rules, continue to the next section to learn how to create custom Hangouts Chat retention rules.

Custom Hangouts Chat retention rules

Chats are a very casual and efficient way for people to communicate as a real-time alternative for sending emails, but this casual style might lead to data leaks, or other potential legal issues.

To set up up a new rule, follow these steps:

1. Define the **Entity** you wish to apply the rule to, as follows:

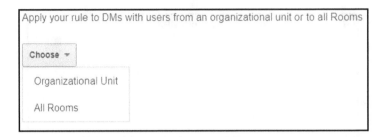

- Select **Organizational Unit** to target direct messages but ignore the rooms
- Select **All Rooms** to target rooms but ignore direct messages

2. Set the **Duration** for this rule; I recommend using **Indefinitely** and changing it later, but only if necessary. This is the number of days that the system will wait before taking action after a message is sent:

Define the **Action after expiration** if you chose a specific number days, as follows:

- **Expunge just the messages that users have already deleted** will only remove messages that have been more there than the days defined by this rule and that have also been deleted by the user. This is recommended to avoid unwanted data loss.
- **Expunge all messages** will remove everything that is older than the specified days. This can be frustrating for users, and might lead to unwanted data loss.

3. Click **SAVE**.

You are ready now to easily set up a custom retention rule for Hangouts Chat. In the next section, you will discover that you already know how to set up custom Hangouts Meet retention rules. Let's find out why.

Custom Hangouts Meet rule

Meet rules are basically a special case of Drive files that the system generates when a user records a Hangouts Meet. The setup process is just like the one we learned about for Drive, but will only apply to these recordings.

Congratulations—you are ready to set up any custom retention rules for G Suite components. Now we know that, it's time to move onto the next section and learn how to put our retained data to work by *Implementing matters*.

Implementing matters

Google Vault uses matters to contain all data related to one investigation by grouping all the information associated with it.

When you are using Vault to search for information, you must do so from within a matter. It will allow you to store and share your findings related to a particular investigation.

You can define the scope of your searches as wide as a whole organization, or narrow it down as much as you need to isolate the information that's needed for the investigation.

My matters

When you find something while searching company data, you can save the query as a matter so that you can use it again later or share it with another authorized user. In other words, since the information is persistently stored in Vault, matters store the queries that are needed to find specific information within Vault so that administrators can review them again later, or share them with other authorized users.

To create a new matter, follow these easy steps:

1. Click **CREATE** on the top-left menu:

2. Write the **Matter name** and **Description** on the form:

3. Click **Create new matter** to finish the setup

Next, send the matter you just created. From within a matter, you can do the following:

1. Create, review, or update holds
2. **Search** through Vault information
3. **Export** Vault records
4. **Audit** Vault usage

These options are all evident in the left-hand side menu, as shown in the following screenshot:

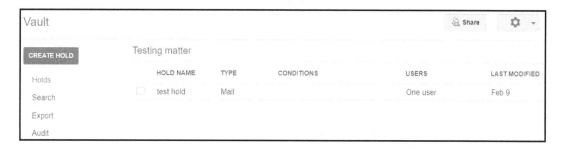

In the next section, we will explore how you can use holds to lock down specific files or messages that are part of an investigation.

Holds

You can create a hold over the data of a user or organizational unit so that Vault keeps that data indefinitely, even if that is past the requirements of any applicable retention rule.

Holds are placed on specific users, or organizational units, to retain their data indefinitely. Holds take precedence over the default retention rule and over any custom retention rules.

To create a new hold, follow these steps:

1. Click **CREATE HOLD** to start
2. Write the **Name** of the hold:

3. Select the **Type** of hold you wish to create

Let's spend some time exploring the different types of holds; we will start by learning how to implement Mail holds in the next section.

Implementing Mail holds

You can set up mail holds that target messages sent within a time period, or that match specific terms defined by search operators.

Defining an email hold is easy. Just follow these steps:

1. In the **User** section, define the following:
    - The **Account** you wish to target:

    - The **Organization** that you wish to target:

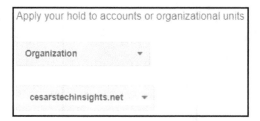

2. Define the conditions for the messages that will be targeted by this hold. These could be any of the following:

- From which **Sent date.**
- To which **Sent date.**
- **Terms** defined by search operator. The following screenshot shows these options:

3. Click **Save** to apply the hold.

Now, all email messages that match your conditions will be placed on permanent hold; remember that if you leave an empty field, it will ignore that filter. For example, if you only define the initial date, all messages after it will be placed on hold.

Sometimes, you will need to target files instead, so continue to the next section to learn how to create Drive holds.

Implementing Drive holds

Drive holds allow administrators to create holds that target all the files within a user's account or an entire organization.

To define a Drive hold, follow these easy steps:

1. At the **User** section, select which of the following you wish to target:
   - Define the targeted **Accounts** in a comma-separated list:

   - Select the **Organization** you wish to target on the drop-down menu:

2. Click **Save** to apply the hold

Now, you are done setting up your Drive hold for that target; there is no need to specify content or dates. Continue to the next section to learn how to implement a Groups hold.

Implementing Groups holds

Creating a Groups hold is similar to setting up a hold for emails, but these are used to target a specific group account, or all group accounts.

To create a Groups hold, follow these easy steps:

1. At the **User** section, select which of the following you wish to target:
   - Specific **Group accounts** separated by a comma, when there are many:

   - **All groups** in the organization

2. Define the conditions for the messages that will be targeted by this hold:

   - From which **Sent date.**
   - To which **Sent date.**
   - **Terms** defined by search operators. The following screenshot shows these options:

3. Click **Save** to apply the hold

By now, you must be getting the hang of how setting up a hold works; let's see how it's done for Hangouts Chat to complete our knowledge on setting up holds.

Implementing Hangouts Chat holds

Setting up a Hangouts Chat hold allows you to target chat conversations for specific accounts or an organization.

Follow these easy steps to create a hold for Hangouts Chats:

1. In the **User** section, define the following:
    *   The **Account** that you wish to target:

    *   The **Organization** that you wish to target:

2. Click **Save** to apply the hold

We just learned how all the different holds are set up, and now that we know how to hold our information for an investigation, let's continue to the next section and learn how to search through the data.

Search

It's time to learn how to search through Vault and narrow down the results until you find what you need for your investigation.

First, you must indicate the kind of search you wish to perform by selecting one of these options on the first drop-down menu:

1. **Mail**, to investigate issues related to email messages. This could be because some member is suspected of sending inappropriate messages, or sharing sensitive information over email.
2. **Drive**, to investigate issues related to files. You might need this to find the source of sensitive files that have been leaked to the public.
3. **Groups**, to investigate messages that have been sent over group email accounts. This might be necessary when there is an issue with something being shared through one of the groups.
4. **Hangouts Chat**, to investigate chat messages.

Let's explore the different search options in the following sections. We will start by learning how to investigate through email messages.

Searching Mail

Vault can search through email messages and also text-based attachment files, like those ending in .doc or .pdf, but be aware that it won't work for video, audio, images, or binary content. The email search page looks as follows:

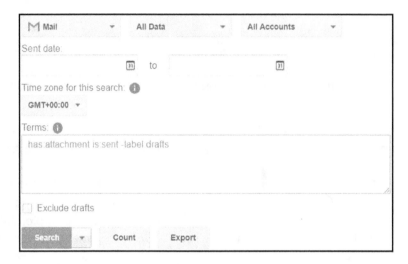

Once you have selected **Mail** as the target for your search, follow these steps:

1. Choose a data source from the **All Data** drop-down menu, as shown in the preceding screenshot. The following is a list of the data source options:
   - **All Data**: Will cover everything available in the organization
   - **Held Data**: Will focus the search on the data that is on litigation hold for the associated matter
   - **Unprocessed Data**: This will use data that is not currently indexed; since it's not processed yet, you cannot use terms to narrow down the results on this data

2. Define the scope for the search from the **All Accounts** drop-down, as shown in the preceding screenshot. The following is the list of options:
   - **All Accounts** will use all accounts that are backed up in Vault within the organization
   - **Specific Accounts** will narrow down the search to one specific user's data
   - **Organizational Unit** will narrow down the search to the user's data within an organizational unit

3. If you need to be more specific, you can filter all messages before or after a certain date, as well as within a date range, by filling the appropriate date range in the **Sent date** and **to** fields.

4. Optionally, you can also define a **Time zone for this search**. You might need this if your team or clients are within different time zones since it can affect a date range.

5. You can also define **Terms** if you need to narrow down your search to very specific content. This is particularly useful when you have too many unnecessary records matching your search.

The next step is to click on the **Search** button, but since the flow is the same for all types, we will continue from that step and beyond when we get to the *Executing search and exporting results* section.

In the next section, you will learn what to do when an investigation requires searching drive files.

Searching Drive

Vault indexes, and is capable of searching through all documents and some types of files, owned or shared directly, to the account of a member of the organization. The Drive search page looks as follows:

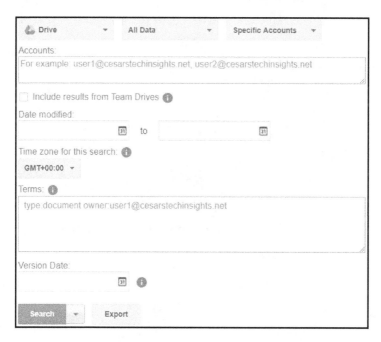

Select **Drive** as the target for your search and follow these steps to define your search:

1. Choose a data source from the **All Data** drop-down menu, as shown in the preceding screenshot. The following is a list of the data source options:
    *   **All Data**: Will cover everything available in the organization
    *   **Held Data**: Will focus the search on the data that is on litigation hold for the associated matter
2. Define the scope for the search from the **Specific Accounts** drop-down, as shown in the preceding screenshot. The following is the list of options:
    *   **Specific Accounts** target a list of one or many comma-separated accounts.
    *   **Organizational Unit** the search will cover all user's data within an organizational unit.
    *   **Team Drives** focuses the search on the files stored within a Team Drive. To use this, follow these steps:
        1. Click **Find Team Drives**
        2. Type in an account that is a member of the Team Drive you wish to target
        3. Click on the name, or press *Enter*:
        4. Click **Next**
        5. Write the name of the team you wish to target
        6. Click on the name, or press *Enter*:

        7. Click **Done** to finish defining the scope of the search

3. Select if you wish the search to also **Include results from team drives**.
4. If you need to be more specific, you can filter all messages before or after a certain date, as well as within a date range, by filling the appropriate date range in the **Sent date** and **to** fields.
5. To refine your search even more, you can define a **Time zone** for this search. You might need this if your team or clients are within different time zones since it can affect a date range.
6. If needed, you can define **Terms**, just like we did when searching Vault Mails.

We will continue with the next steps when we talk about *Executing search and exporting results*; in the next section, you will learn how *Searching Groups* messages works.

Searching Groups

Searching through Groups is much like what we did for Mails, but this will be focused on Groups instead of accounts or organizational units. The Groups search page looks as follows:

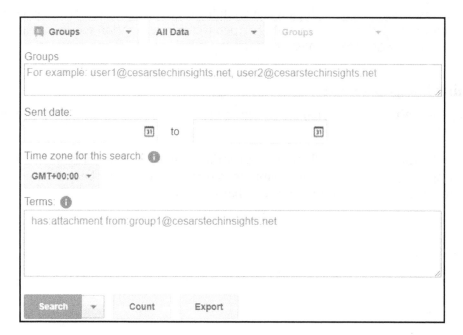

If you selected **Groups** as the target for your search, follow these steps to define it:

1. Choose a data source from the **All Data** drop-down menu, as shown in the preceding screenshot. The following is a list of the data source options:
   - **All Data**: Will cover everything available in the organization
   - **Held Data**: Will focus the search on the data that is on litigation hold for the associated matter
   - **Unprocessed Data**: This will use data that is not currently indexed, and since it's not processed yet, you cannot use terms to narrow down the results on this data

2. You can optionally filter all messages before or after a certain date, as well as within a date range, by filling the appropriate date range in the **Sent date** and **to** fields.

3. Furthermore, you can define a **Time zone** for this search if your team or clients are within different time zones.

4. Finally, you can also define **Terms**, just like we did for the other search types.

We will continue with the next steps when we talk about *Executing search and exporting results*, but for now, let's see what would happen if our investigation requires searching Hangouts Chat messages in the next section.

Searching Hangouts Chat

Searching through Hangouts Chat allows you to investigate chat messages from members of the domain.

When investigating Hangouts Chat, the appropriate use of specific terms is usually the key to narrowing things down to a manageable search result. You might be in the need to try a few different combinations before finding what you need.

The **Hangouts Chat** search page looks as follows:

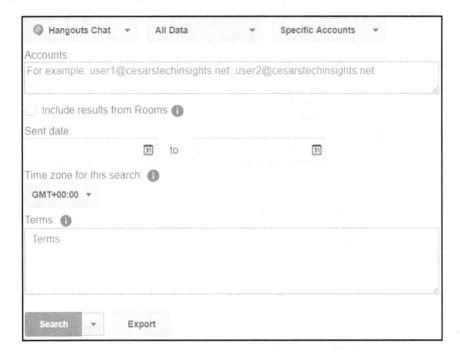

If **Chat** is the target for your search, follow these steps to define it:

1. Choose a data source from the **All Data** drop-down menu, as shown in the preceding screenshot. The following is a list of the data source options:
   - **All Data**: Will cover everything available in the organization
   - **Held Data**: Will focus the search on the data that is on litigation hold for the associated matter
   - **Unprocessed Data**: This will use data that is not currently indexed, since it's not processed yet, you cannot use terms to narrow down the results on this data

2. Define the scope for the search from the **Specific Accounts** drop-down, as shown in the preceding screenshot. The following is the list of options:

- **All accounts** target all the users within the domain.
- **Specific accounts** target a list of one or many comma-separated accounts.
- **Organizational unit** makes the search cover all user's data within an organizational unit.
- **Rooms** focuses the search on the messages within a specific chat room. To do this, follow these steps:
    1. Click **Find Rooms**
    2. Type an account that is a member of the chat room you wish to target
    3. Click on the name, or press *Enter*:

4. Click **Next**
5. Write the name of the team you wish to target
6. Click on the name, or press *Enter*:

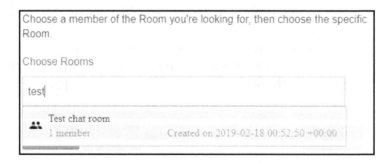

7. Click **Done** to finish defining the scope of the search

3. Select if you wish the search to also **Include results from Team Drives**.
4. You can optionally filter all messages before or after a certain date, as well as within a date range, by filling the appropriate date range in the **Sent date** and **to** fields.
5. You can optionally define a **Time zone** for this search. You might need this if you team or clients are within different time zones since it can affect a date range.
6. You can also define **Terms**, just like we did when searching Vault Mails.

This was the last kind of search that Vault offers, so continue to the next section to learn how to execute your search, and how to manage the results.

Executing search and exporting results

You now know how to set up default and custom data holds that are required for an investigation, and learned how to set up a search for the different types of content within Vault. It is now time to actually search and export our results.

For Mail and Groups searches, the dataset can be large, and processing can take a while. Sometimes, it takes some refinements before finding the right combination to find the information you need. Before you start searching, it's a good idea to click **Count** to verify how many records match your parameters, in case there are too few or too many:

After requesting a search count, you will be able to see the number of records and accounts that matched your criteria. If you need more details, click the **Download accounts with matches** to get a CSV file that details all the account names, and how many records matched each one.

If you click the **Export** button, you will skip the part where you see the results, and the system will start working on the export file immediately; you can track the progress and see the results on the **Export** tab on the left menu. The **Search**, **Count**, and **Export** buttons look as follows:

The arrow next to the **Search** button shows a drop-down menu that allows you to do the following:

- **Reset** all current parameters on the form.
- Create a **Duplicate search form** below the one you are using, with the same parameters. This is useful when investigating and you wish to keep a copy of some search parameters, but keep experimenting with changes.

To see the results, click **Search**, and once the system finishes, you will be taken to the results screen. Let's explore what it has to show us:

- At the top of your results, you will see the **Save query** button, which allows you to keep a copy of the parameters you used to discover something. After you click this button, follow these steps:
    1. Assign a name for this query in the form:

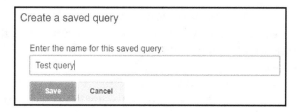

2. Click **Save** to create a quick link below **Search** on the left menu:

- The next button is the **Export results**, which allows you to put your findings on a special file. After you click the button, follow these steps:
    1. Write a name for your search on the **Export name** field:

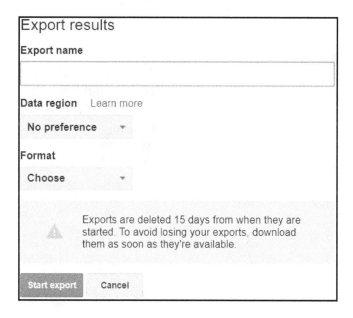

2. You can optionally assign a **Data region** so that your Vault information is physically stored. This could be a legal requirement in some cases. You can choose from the following in the drop-down menu:

- **No preference**: This is the default and Google will place data where they consider it to be more efficient
- **United States**: This will force data to be stored only on data centers located in the United States
- **Europe**: This will force data to be stored only on data centers located in Europe

3. Choose the **Format** of the exported file from the following in the drop-down menu:

- **MBOX**:
  - Used by Mozilla Thunderbird, but can also be seen on a text editor.
  - Can be up to 10 GB in size. If more is needed, multiple files will be created.
  - Each file only holds information from one account. If multiple accounts are in the export, then one file will be created for each account.

- **PST**:
  - Used by Microsoft Outlook.
  - Can be up to 1 GB in size. If more is needed, multiple files will be created.
  - Each file only holds information from one account. If multiple accounts are in the export, then one file will be created for each account.

4. Click **Start export** so that Vault begins building the necessary files to hold the results.

- At the top right, you will see the **Share** button. Use this to share this search with another user. The **Sharing Settings** screen looks as follows:

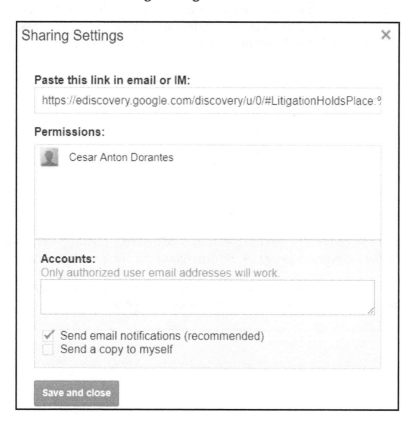

The time it takes the system to build an export file will depend on the amount of information that will be exported; however, you can keep track of its progress and download it once it's ready in the **Export** section of the left menu. We will see more about this in the next few pages.

Now that we have fully covered how to export Mail search results, let's learn how to do it if you need to export Drive search results.

Exporting results

Export allows you to put all the search result information within a file that can be used for legal requirements. Since these files can be substantially large, they might take some time to be processed. The link to **Export** looks as follows on the **Vault** page:

When you export search results, the file creation is added to a queue. Select **Export** on the left menu to review an export's progress, or download the files when ready.

It's important that you download the results as soon as they are ready, since Vault will only hold export files for 15 days. In-progress exports look as follows:

Once an export is ready, will see the following options:

- **View completed files**: Click this to show all downloadable file names and their sizes on a list:
    - Click **Download** next to its name to get a physical copy of the file
- **Show query**: Click this to show the parameters that were used for these results
- **Run query**: Click this to run the query again
- **Show options**: Click this to show the options that were applied to these results

Additionally, you will see these columns for each export:

- **EXPORTED BY**: Shows the name of the person that requested these export files
- **COUNT**: The number of files available within this export
- **SIZE**: The total size of all files within this export
- **DAYS UNTIL EXPORT FILES ARE DELETED**: The days before the results are deleted by Vault

Now, you can export the results for a search within the investigation of a matter. Congratulations, you can now start using Vault to help investigating legal issues related to a G Suite domain, and meet legal requirements for business data retention.

At the bottom of Vault's left menu, you will find the **Reports** section. We will learn about what it can show us in the next section.

Understanding Reports

At this point, you have learned how to use Vault's **Retention** and **Matters**, so it's time for you to learn about what can be found at the bottom of the menu, that is **Reports**:

The **Reports** menu contains the **Audit** tool and also reports for the current **Domain Holds**, **Users Holds**, and **Group Holds**.

To open a report, click on the name, and you will see a list of the active elements for that category. To download a copy of the information within a report, click on the **Download CSV** button on the top right corner.

Since Vault has access to sensitive information, it logs every action on it as a security measure. **Audit** is a special tool that allows you to filter and download all the actions that are performed by administrators inside Vault:

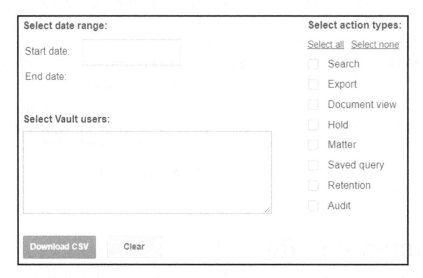

To perform an audit, observe the following steps:

1. **Select date range** that you wish to audit. Leaving the **Start date** empty will target up to the oldest records. Likewise, leaving the **End date** empty will target up to the newest records. If no period is selected, all records will be targeted, regardless of date.
2. **Select Vault users** that you wish to audit. If no user is provided, all users will be targeted.
3. **Select action types** that you wish to audit. Selecting nothing is the same as selecting everything.
4. Click **Download CSV**.

It is important to be aware that audit results are delivered directly as a CSV file instead of being shown in a table or chart. To make it easier to read the file, you can import it into a Google Spreadsheet so that you can sort, search, or add charts.

Audit files contain the following columns:

- `Epoch milliseconds`: This is the date in milliseconds, and is used mostly when exporting to software, for example, `1549071076708`
- `Date`: The is the date in a human readable format, for example `Fri, 01 Feb 2019 17:31:15 -0800`
- `Action`: The label of that action, for example, `ADD_RETENTION_RULE_BEGIN`
- `User`: Email address of the user
- `Matter`: The ID of the matter that the user interacted with
- `Name`: Additional information that's usually describing the target of the action, like the ID of a file
- `Email`: Email of a collaboration that was added or removed from a matter
- `Resource url`: URL of the document that was viewed
- `Query string`: The query parameters that are used for a search
- `Organization`: When the record was related to an organizational unit, you can see it here
- `Details`: The number or days set for a retention rule

With this, you are ready to start reviewing reports about Vault's usage, and with this, you have completed your walk through Vault's features and setups.

Summary

Congratulations on finishing another chapter! You have just learned how to prepare the domain to comply with legal requirements while facing or performing an investigation.

You are now capable of setting the default retention rules on this domain to define the minimum data retention period for the different G Suite components.

In this chapter, you also learned how to make Vault keep an eye out for messages or documents that match specific criteria, and apply a custom retention rule so that these records are kept for a longer period of time than others, or kept indefinitely.

We learned how to implement matters to group all the information that might be relevant to an investigation and how to use them to apply data holds to guarantee that those records will be kept for as long as necessary.

You now know how to search through the information that's held within a matter to find Drive documents, Mail, Group, or Hangouts Chat messages, as well as saving, sharing, and exporting the result of an investigation.

Now that you know how to prepare and perform internal investigations using Google Vault, it's time to continue to the next chapter and learn how to set up the security center.

Further reading

- **How retention works** (https://support.google.com/vault/answer/2990828?hl=enref_topic=3209998)
- **Organize and create matters** (https://support.google.com/vault/answer/2462419)
- **Use search operators** (https://support.google.com/vault/answer/2474474)
- **Get started with search and export** (https://support.google.com/vault/answer/6161352?hl=en)
- **Importing and exporting your mail** (http://kb.mozillazine.org/Importing_and_exporting_your_mail)

Section 3: Security, Privacy, and Troubleshooting

In this section, you will learn how to set up, manage, and analyze your security to prevent, find, and fix any security problems in G Suite.

The following chapter is included in this section:

- Chapter 8, *Setting Up Security*

Setting Up Security

8

G Suite is built with a security-first mindset. It's designed to meet the highest security standards and is subject to regular independent third-party audits by several national and international agencies and organizations.

One key difference between the free and business versions is the security features. Free accounts are not designed to be handled individually, so there is no easy way to monitor or enforce security.

Business accounts, on the other hand, allow administrators to enforce advanced security like two-step verification and login challenges to prevent attacks, even when some user credentials are compromised.

The **Security** center allows administrators to easily adjust all settings related to domain security and user account protection. The& **Security** center is divided into different sections, each showing its name and a short description. To access these sections, simply click on it and it will unfold its contents.

In this chapter, we will learn how to do the following:

- Identify and configure the different options for two-step verification flow
- Monitor a user's password strength
- Configure login challenges
- Enable the Admin SDK and identify its use
- Set up **single sign-on (SSO)**
- Define the user session limit

Basic settings

The **Basic settings** section provides administrators with quick access to the **Password Recovery** flow, as well as links for setting up **Two-step verification** and user's access to **Less secure apps**.

Enabling the **Two-step verification (2SV)** login flow will require the user to provide a key coming from a registered device in addition to their username and password. Each generated key is only usable once, so without the device, the credentials are not enough to access the account.

You can choose any of the following options for two-step authentication:

- **Security Keys** that are provided by special devices, usually USB drives that one physically inserts in the machine, or sometimes it's a card that you tap to a **Near Field Communication** (**NFC**) or **Bluetooth Low Energy** (**BLE**) device. This is the safest option, but also more expensive to implement.
- A **Google Prompt** that shows on the user's Android or Apple device to confirm a login attempt. This is a very effective and easy-to-use way of doing this.
- Using the **Google Authenticator** app. This is a special application that generates single-use 2SV keys. This is basically a software version of a security key generator, so there is no need to buy specialized hardware. This is a very safe and cost-effective option.

The **Two-step verification** settings looks as follows:

To implement **Two-step verification**, follow these steps:

1. Enable **Allow users to turn on 2-step verification**.
2. Click **SAVE** to apply changes. Optionally, you can define more details by following these steps:
    1. Click **Go to advanced settings to enforce 2-step verification**
    2. If you are handling more than one organization, you can select the one that you wish to set up these rules by selecting the name on the left menu:

3. To set up a **Group Filter** to grant this privilege to only a specific part of the organization, follow these steps:

    1. Click **SELECT** on the bottom left menu:

    2. Click on the group you wish to enable direct access to password recovery:

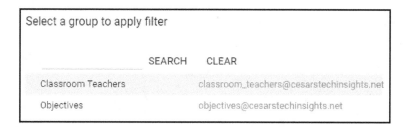

    3. Click **DONE** to apply the filter. You can see the targeted users at the top of the setup options:

4. Define the **2-step verification Enforcement** policy for this group by selecting one of these options:

- Apply the enforcement after a certain date by selecting it on **Turn on enforcement from date**:
  - Click **enrollment report** to see a report of this policy compliance by the users
- **Turn on enforcement now** will apply two-step verification immediately
- **Turn off enforcement** so users are never required to use it

5. Select how much time new accounts can go after activation before being required to use two-step verification on the **New user enrollment period** drop-down menu:

6. Select the **Allowed 2-step verification method**:
  1. Choose **Any** to allow users to use a physical key and all web security flows
  2. Choose **Only Security Key** to require users to use a special physical security device to access:

- Select a **2-step verification policy suspension grace period**, which is a period that administrators give to users to be able to access using other security flows, usually while they are given a new key

7. Select the **2-step verification frequency**to define if users can log in only once on selected devices, or whether they should always follow the 2SV

8. At the **Password recovery** section, you can **Enable non-admin user password recovery**to allow users that are not administrators to perform **Password recovery** so that they can regain access to their accounts without the help of an administrator:

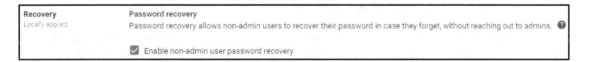

9. Click **SAVE** on the bottom left corner to persist changes

As an administrator, you can define whether the users within the domain can install additional apps, even if they are using a less secure sign-in technology, although this is not recommended. You can do this by following these steps:

1. Click **Go to settings for less secure apps**, as follows:

Less secure apps Locally applied	◉ Disable access to less secure apps for all users (Recommended) ◯ Allow users to manage their access to less secure apps ◯ Enforce access to less secure apps for all users (Not Recommended) Some apps use less secure sign-in technology, which makes accounts more vulnerable. You can choose to deny access for these apps, which we recommend, or choose to allow access despite the risks. ❷

Select the restriction level for **Less secure apps**. The options are outlined as follows:

- **Disable access to less secure apps for all users** is the recommended option and will completely prevent less secure apps to be used in the domain.
- **Allow users to manage their access to less secure apps** will allow administrators to allow specific apps. Use this only if you really need to use a specific app.
- **Enforce access to less secure apps** for all users will allow the free use of less secure applications, although this is not recommended.

2. Click **SAVE** on the bottom right corner to apply your changes.

By setting up the basic settings, you have quickly covered the most crucial configurations, but there is still much more to cover; continue to the next section to learn how to set up **Password management**.

Password management

Having a strong password is essential to keep an account safe; even the strongest encryption can't offer much protection if the key is easy to figure out.

As a G Suite administrator, you can enforce requirements for all passwords within the organization. This helps set a minimum security strength that's required for all accounts.

To set up password requirements, follow these steps:

1. Having a strong security protocol is not effective if the password strength is weak and therefore easy to guess. You can be sure all user's passwords are inline with current best practices by enabling the **Enforce strong password** checkbox:

2. By defining a **Password length**, you can be sure that user's passwords are not too short, but keep in mind that passwords below eight characters are not recommended:

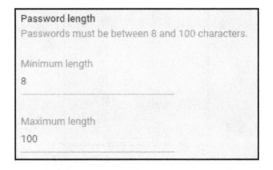

3. To avoid existing users from keeping a low security password, you can enable **Start password policy enforcement at next sign in** so that everyone without a strong password will be required to change it the next time they log in:

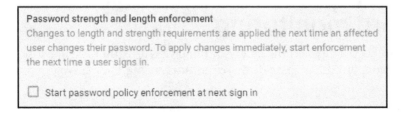

4. Always using the same password can be easy for the user, but it makes the account more vulnerable. Disable **Allow password reuse** to prevent users from keeping the same password, even after a change request:

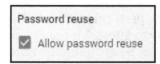

5. Keeping the same password for too long can make the account vulnerable; define the **Password expiration** to a reasonable length so that your users don't keep the same password for too long. The recommended length is **90 days** to keep things safe without being too hard on your users:

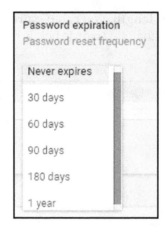

You can now define the password requirements for members of this organization. In the next section, we will learn what **Password monitoring** can teach us about our user's passwords.

Password monitoring

It's important to keep an eye on the safety of the passwords that are used by the members of the organization, but it has to be done without us seeing the passwords themselves.

In **Password monitoring**, you can quickly overlook the current strength and length of, all of your member's passwords as shown in the following screenshot:

NAME	PASSWORD LENGTH	PASSWORD STRENGTH
Cesar Anton Dorantes	13	
Rudolph Almeida	8	

If you believe that a user should set a new password, follow these steps:

1. Click on the user's name. This will take you to that user's account details, as shown here:

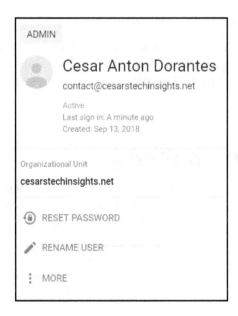

2. Select if you wish the system to automatically generate a temporary password. If you disable it, you need to provide one yourself:

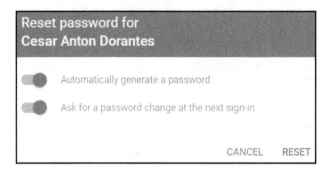

3. Select if you wish the user to be required to change the password at their next sign in.
4. Click **RESET** to apply any changes.

In this section, you learned how to monitor a user's password characteristics, and even request them to use another password if the current one is not safe enough. To increase security, you can also define **Login challenges** to complement the passwords. You will learn how to do this in the next section.

Defining login challenges

G Suite can detect unusual login attempts to user accounts; you can enable additional **Login challenges** that the system will use on these cases to reduce the risk of unauthorized access using compromised login credentials. The **Login challenges** settings are as follows:

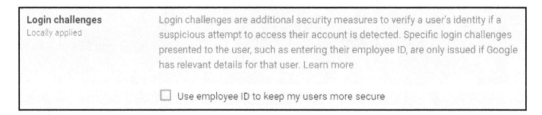

There are three types of login challenges in G Suite:

- **Mobile device challenges**: These use a physical mobile device that the user has registered as their own as a source of truth for confirming the login attempt. If the user has a registered device verification, it can be done in one of three possible ways:
    - A **prompt** that will show up on the mobile device for the user to confirm the login attempt. I find this to be the most practical option.
    - A **text message** with a verification code that the user must type as proof.
    - A **phone call** with a verification code on a voice message that the user must type as proof.
- **Employee ID login challenge**: The user will be asked to type their employee ID to confirm their identity.
- **Recovery email challenge**: The user will be asked to type their recovery email address to confirm their identity.

You just learned how to set up the login challenges; these will be very useful for your users to be able to quickly fix many security issues without requiring the aid of an administrator, saving both time and frustration.

Let's continue to the next section to learn when to enable **API access** and learn about the **Admin SDK**.

Enabling API access

An organization can extend G Suite by enabling API access so that developers can create software that integrates with the services and optimize the way things work to best suit the organization's needs.

API access is required for external applications to integrate with G Suite. Keeping it disabled will prevent all users from installing third-party applications, so it's a good idea to turn it off unless it's necessary to keep things safer. You can use the **Enable API access** checkbox to enable or disable API access:

The administrator's console also has an API that allows developers to extend and customize it for the organization's needs so that it can facilitate the administrator's tasks.

The **Admin SDK** settings can also be found on the same page:

> Admin SDK
> The Google Admin SDK allows developers to write applications to manage your Cloud Directory, migrate from and integrate with existing IT infrastructure, create users, update settings, audit activity, and more.

The Admin SDK allows organizations to build tools tailored to their very unique need; you will learn how to your own custom tools in the next chapter, but before that, let's continue to the next section to learn how to *Set up single sign-on (SSO)*.

Set up single sign-on (SSO)

Business grade sign-in flows are highly reliable, and in many cases, users will need to use other web applications. Managing several high security credentials at the same time can be too cumbersome for users.

With SSO, members of the organization can use their G Suite credentials to safely identify themselves on third-party applications.

To configure SSO, follow the appropriate steps, depending on whether you will be using Google identity provider or a third-party service:

- **Setup SSO with Google identity provider**. To use Google credentials for SSO, follow these steps:
    1. Copy the **SSO URL** or the **Entity ID**. This will be used by the applications to get the login information:

    2. Click **DOWNLOAD CERTIFICATE**.
    3. Click **DOWNLOAD IDP METADATA:**

    4. Register the information that was gathered in steps *1*, *2*, and *3* into the third-party service providers.

- To use a custom identity provider, enable **Setup SSO with third party identity provider**, and then follow these steps:
    1. Type the external **Sign-in page URL**.
    2. Type the external **Sign-out page URL**.

3. Type the external **Change password URL**. Users who are not administrators of this domain will be taken to the following page:

To setup third party as your identity provider, please provide the information below.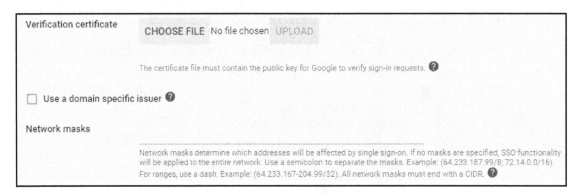

Sign-in page URL

URL for signing in to your system and G Suite

Sign-out page URL

URL for redirecting users to when they sign out

Change password URL

URL to let users change their password in your system; when defined here, this is shown even when Single Sign-on is not enabled

4. Click **CHOOSE FILE.**
5. Upload the **Verification certificate**.
6. Use a domain-specific issuer.
7. If you need to target only specific IPs, you can define a **Network mask**; if none are provided, SSO will be globally applied. Several network masks are possible by separating them with a semicolon.

These settings can be seen in the following screenshot:

Verification certificate

CHOOSE FILE   No file chosen   UPLOAD

The certificate file must contain the public key for Google to verify sign-in requests.

☐ Use a domain specific issuer

Network masks

Network masks determine which addresses will be affected by single sign-on. If no masks are specified, SSO functionality will be applied to the entire network. Use a semicolon to separate the masks. Example: (64.233.187.99/8; 72.14.0.0/16). For ranges, use a dash. Example: (64.233.167-204.99/32). All network masks must end with a CIDR.

With SSO, the organization can use a single identity provider across all applications, so they only need to log in once, and the session will be valid for all approved applications.

In the next section, you will learn about Google session control and how it can help you control how often users need to sign in.

Setting up Google session control

At this point, you already know how to apply the different configurations that will allow users to safely log in to the platform. Users will only be active for a few hours, and then will not return until the next day.

Leaving a Google session active for too long without being used is an unnecessary risk, and to minimize this, G Suite allows administrators to define how long a session is considered valid. After this period, the user will be required to log in again.

To define the session length, click on the **Session control** drop-down menu and select the amount of hours it will last. It can be as short as one hour, or as long as 30 days. You can even make sessions never expire:

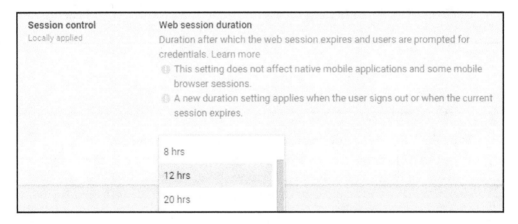

Ideally, a session should last an entire day. In most cases, 12 hours should be enough for a user to only be required to log in at the beginning a working day.

Being able to define a session length allows you to easily reduce the chance of unauthorized access. Continue to the next section to learn how you can manage API client access.

Configuring Advanced settings

As an administrator, you can whitelist the address of specific web applications that are authorized to access specific G Suite APIs for this domain. This way, you can make sure that only authorized applications can use APIs. To make things even safer, administrators can define the approved scope for each application.

To authorize an application to have API access, follow these steps in the **Advanced settings** section:

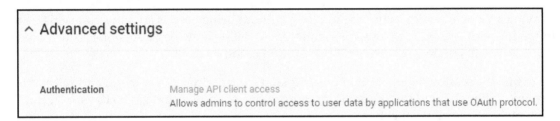

1. Click on **Manage API client access** and go to the authorized API clients list:

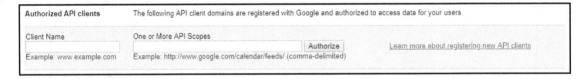

2. Type the URL of the application in the **Client Name** field.
3. Type the API scopes (separated by a comma) that this application is authorized to access in the **One or More API Scopes** field. To see a full list of all currently available APIs and scopes, go to `https://developers.google.com/identity/protocols/googlescopes`.
4. Click **Authorize**.

By defining the API client authorizations, you help prevent unauthorized people from using the APIs. By delimiting each client scope, you know exactly how much access is given to any application.

You can now whitelist applications that are allowed to integrate with G Suite on this domain. In the next section, you will learn how to set up API permissions.

Setting up API permissions

When external apps try to access your team's data, they must first have explicit authorization to access this information.

Each G Suite product and service has a separate API, and as an administrator, you can choose which APIs can be made accessible to external apps. The settings for each G Suite product look as follows:

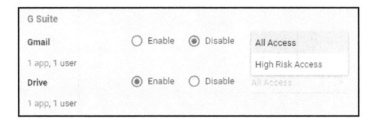

At the bottom of the API lists, you can see the links to **Installed Apps** and the **Trusted Apps** reports. Continue to the next section to see what we can learn about the **Installed Apps** report.

Installed Apps

The **Installed Apps** report shows you all the applications that are currently allowed and being used by members of the organization. You can also review which kind of information they have access to, as shown in the following screenshot:

You can use the **Filters panel** to narrow down the list of apps in the reports, and you can filter by the following settings:

- **API Permission**: This will only show applications that have access to a specific API:

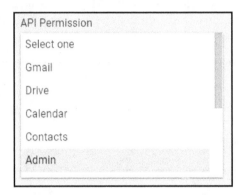

- **App Name**: Use this if you know the name of the application you are looking for:

- **User Count**: This allows you to filter applications, depending on the amount of users it has in this domain:

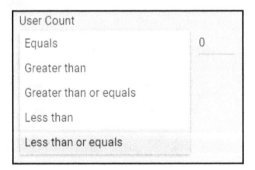

The **Installed Apps** report allows you to analyze which third-party applications are being used within the domain. In the next section, we will explore the **Trusted Apps** report.

Trusted Apps

As an administrator, you can whitelist applications that are allowed to be used within the organization by adding them to this list.

Trusted versus installed apps:
The **trusted apps report** will show the applications that users can install in this domain.
The **installed apps report** will show the applications that users in this domain has installed.

In this section, we will learn how to whitelist the applications that are authorized to integrate with this domain. The **TRUSTED** apps list looks as follows:

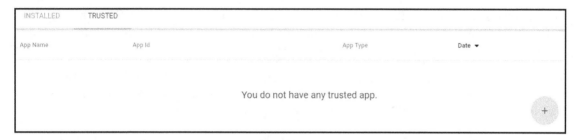

To add a new trusted app, follow these steps:

1. Select **App Type**:
   - **Web Application**, **Android**, or **iOS**

2. Select the app you wish to whitelist:
   - For web applications, type the OAuth2 Client ID, and then click **ADD**
   - For **iOS** and **Android** apps, just type the name of the app you are looking for and then follow these steps:
     1. Click **Search**
     2. Select the app
     3. Click **ADD**

By carefully setting API permissions, you can validate and control the data that's accessible by external applications that integrate with G Suite.

Summary

Congratulations on finishing this chapter! You have just learned how to set up the security settings for a G Suite domain to fit the particular needs of your organization.

In this chapter, you learned how to set up two-step authentication to protect user accounts with advanced login security. This was followed by password requirements across the entire organization, as well as how to monitor a user's password strength, which is key to bolstering organizational security.

You also learned how to enable the Admin SDK to allow third-party software to integrate with G Suite. Furthermore, we also covered how to set up SSO so that users can use the same user session across all their applications.

We closed this chapter by discussing how to set up API permissions to define which third-party applications can integrate with G Suite for this domain, as well as what information is accessible for each individual application.

With this chapter, we finish our journey of the main parts of G Suite, and you are prepared to start implementing it on organizations. You can start practicing by creating an account for your business, or a professional account for yourself.

But we are not done yet. At this point, you know how to set up the main administrator tools that come with G Suite, so let's take this one step further and learn how use Google Sites to create sites and web applications that can seamlessly integrate with G Suite, and even external portals like Twitter.

Further reading

- **Protect your business with 2-Step Verification** (https://support.google.com/a/answer/175197?hl=en)
- **Create a strong password & a more secure account** (https://support.google.com/accounts/answer/32040)
- **Verify a user's identity with extra security** (https://support.google.com/a/answer/6002699?hl=en)
- **Set up single sign-on for managed Google Accounts using third-party Identity providers** (https://support.google.com/a/answer/60224)
- **If you have multiple G Suite subscriptions** (https://support.google.com/a/answer/6274252?hl=en)
- **Whitelist connected apps** (https://support.google.com/a/answer/7281227)

Section 4: Apps and Sites

4

In this section, you will learn how to create apps that seamlessly integrate with your G Suite tools and services.

The following chapter is included in this section:

- Chapter 9, *Getting Started with Google Sites*

Getting Started with Google Sites

9

The Information Age is changing the way we live, work, and do business. The rising expectations to be considered competitive on a global market requires professionals and organizations to use more sophisticated marketing tools.

Having a website is becoming a basic necessity in today's market. Websites give professionals and corporations online presence and act as the bridge between customers and businesses.

Google Sites offers a very intuitive way to create websites. Adding elements—such as pictures or videos—requires only a few clicks, and they can be rearranged by simply dragging them. If you have created a presentation before with Google Slides, you will find that creating a website is not very different from this.

Google Sites also includes the same real-time collaboration features that you have in Google Drive tools, such as Docs, Slides, and Sheets. This makes creating and maintaining a website much easier and cheaper, especially since collaborators don't require programming skills.

All the components are designed to be responsive by default, so you don't need to worry about creating special designs for each kind of device.

To make things better, Sites comes with a very easy and powerful tool that allows you to preview an emulated version of your site on mobile, tablet, and large-screen devices with a single click.

In this chapter, you will learn about the following topics:

- Creating a new site
- Adding content to a site
- Adding pages and navigation to a site
- Publishing a site
- Assigning a custom URL to a site
- Integrating sites and documents

Creating new sites

With Google Sites, organizations are not limited to creating a single site for the entire organization; sites can be created as much as needed, and they can be used for public purposes, such as promoting a new product, or for private ones, such as documentation and reports.

To access Google Sites, open `https://sites.google.com` on a browser tab. The Google Sites home screen allows you to access your current site projects by selecting them from the list, or to create new ones with a single click:

Instead of creating a PDF and sending a report by email, you can create a private website that will always be showing the latest reports, and doesn't worry about security and access management; it works just like Google Drive.

If you created a new account at the beginning of this book, that means you have no sites for this account yet, so let's create one by clicking the **Create new site** icon on the bottom-right corner:

This will create a new **Untitled Site**, as shown in the following screenshot:

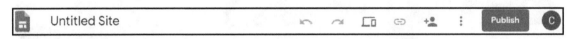

Let's explore the main components from the top menu, from left to right:

- Click ![] to go back to your sites list.
- Click **Untitled Site**. Type the name of the site you are creating.
- Click ![] to undo your last action.
- Click ![] to cancel the last undo.
- Click ![] to see a preview of the site for mobiles, tablets, and large screens.
- Click ![] to share the site project with other G Suite users. It works even with free account users.
- Click **PUBLISH** to launch the site.

Now that our site has a name, let's give it a theme by following these steps:

1. Click **Themes** on the right-hand side menu
2. Select a theme you like:

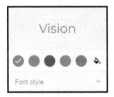

3. Select an accent color
4. Select a **Font style**

To give it a more personal touch, let's change the image at the header of the site:

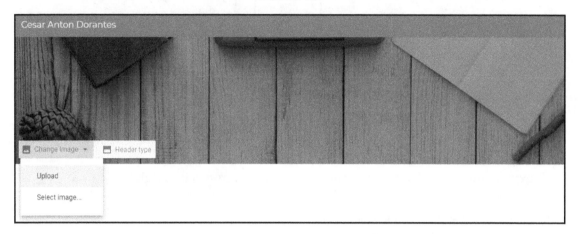

Click on **Change Image** and select a source for the new background by using one of the following options:

- **Upload** to use a file stored on the device
- **Select Image...** to use images from the web or drive

Now, let's select a header type we like for our site:

- Select **Cover** to use a very tall header
- Select **Large banner** to use a tall header
- Select **Banner** to use a normal header
- Select **Title only** to show the title without images

In this section, you learned how to create new sites and how to apply a theme and style; new pages of your site will also have the elements we defined in this section by default. This will make it easier to keep the site consistent.

Now, it's time for you to start adding content, so continue to the next section to learn how.

Adding content

Google Sites makes it very easy to add new content on a site, as each page of a site is build by elements arranged vertically: at the top you will find the logo, name of the site, and the navigation menu, followed by the (optional) header of your site.

Only the header is static; below it, you can use as many elements as you find necessary. Elements on a site will be placed one on top of the another, and you can change the order by simply dragging the element to the position where you want it to be.

 Each element covers the entire width of the site; this allows it to easily adapt to small devices, such as mobiles, in a vertical position.

In sites, you can simply insert elements on the site and then adjust them as needed. You will need a text box to show the welcome message; follow these steps to create one:

1. Click **Insert** on the right-hand side menu:

2. Click the **Text box** button on the **Insert** menu. This will add a text element at the top of the body:

3. Click on the text box that you just created; you will find it below the header:

4. Type in the message you want to appear.

5. Use the top menu to adjust the text properties to your liking.

You can easily add text and images, or if you want to mix them on a single element, choose one of the section layout options.

The **Insert** menu comes with the components we need to easily create a website; just click on something you want to add, set it up, and drag elements to be in the order you want them.

You can also embed pieces of code into your site. This allows you to easily integrate your site with platforms such as Twitter. To see how this works, follow these steps to add a Twitter timeline to your site:

1. Open a new browser tab

2. Go to `https://publish.twitter.com/`

3. Write the URL of the Twitter account you wish to share:

4. Press *Enter* or click the arrow on the right

5. Click **Embedded Timeline**

6. Click **Copy Code**

7. Go back to your Google Sites project

8. Click the **Embed** button on the **Insert** menu:

9. Click on the **Embed code** tab

10. Paste the code we received in step *6*

11. Click **Next**

12. Confirm that the correct timeline appears

13. Click **Insert** to add the timeline to your site

Now, a timeline of the account you chose will be available on this site; this shows you how easy it is to integrate your site with external services.

 You can easily add payments to a Google Site by using PayPal buttons. These include **Shopping cart**, **Buy now**, **Donations**, **Subscriptions**, **Automatic billing**, and **Installment plan**. This way, you can create a catalog of products and services and be able to sell them directly from your site, no coding needed.

Each element that you add to the site will have its own section, and these can be moved and styled independently:

Hover over a section to see the available options for it.

To move a section drag (click and hold) it from the vertical dots on the left, and place it where you want it to go.

Add some styling to our timeline by following these steps:

1. Hover over the section and click on the **Section background** icon:

2. Click **Emphasis 1** to make it stand out a little

To make better use of our site space, let's split the space of the body horizontally so that we can put the Twitter timeline next to the welcome message. To do that, follow these steps:

1. Click the **Divider** button on the **Insert** menu
2. Drag the timeline to the center of its section:

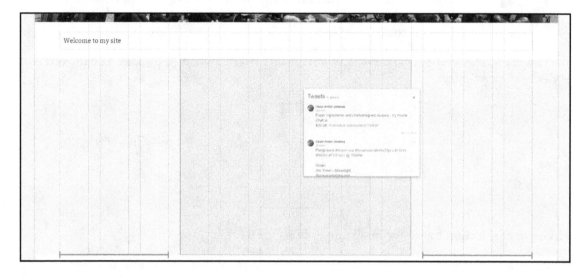

While dragging an element, you will see the site's grid lines; these will make it easier to properly align your site.

Now, you know how to add different kinds of content to a page, but Google Sites doesn't limit you to a single-page application, so continue to the next section to learn how to add more pages to your site.

Adding pages

To avoid adding too much content to a single page, you can add more pages to your site. Luckily, adding more pages to your site is very easy too.

Using multiple pages also makes it easier for visitors to find specific content; if they like a product, they can simply bookmark it so that they can return later.

To add more pages to your site, follow these steps:

1. Click **Pages** on the right-hand side menu.

2. Hover over the add button 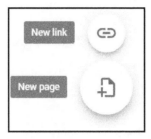 to show all the available options:

3. Click **New page**.
4. Write the name of the new page. Let's create one called YouTube videos.

You will be taken to the new page that will already have the header, and a navigation menu will also be added automatically. You can click on a page on the navigation menu to edit that section. All the changes you do are saved automatically, so you can easily change between sections and edit them as needed.

You can also use the previous steps to add links to external sites; these can be to your social networks, or any public link you wish.

If you hover over the name of the section you just created, you will see the options icon; let's explore what you can do here:

- **Make homepage**: Click this to define this page as the starting point for new visitors.
- **Duplicate page**: Click this to make a copy of this page at the same level; this will allow you to easily reuse the style of one page, which is very useful when building catalogs or reports.
- **Properties**: This allows you to change the name or set a custom URL for this page.

- **Add subpage**: This is a very powerful option that allows you to create pages within pages—for example, you can create a sub-page for each YouTube video instead of having them all together. You can use this to create entire catalogs as big and as complex as you need.
- **Hide from navigation**: This will make the page accessible to visitors, but other collaborators will still be able to work on it. This way, you can publish the pages that are ready and hold the ones that are still a work in progress.
- **Delete**: This will permanently delete this page.

Our new page is now empty. In the last section, we learned how to add and embed content, so let's try something different and learn how to add a YouTube video to this page by following these steps:

1. Click **Insert** on the right-hand side menu:

2. Click the YouTube button on the **Insert** menu:

3. Write the name of the video you want to add.
4. Click the search button.
5. Click on the video you want to add. If you want to share more than one, just select many videos, as this will create a new section for each video and will save you the need to create them one by one.
6. Click **Select** once you are done choosing videos.

7. Drag each video to center it on its element:

We now have a basic site, but before publishing the site, follow these steps to preview it:

1. Click  to launch the preview:

2. Use the menu on the bottom right to toggle between the available views: **Phone**, **Tablet**, and **Large screen**. You will notice that your site is already responsive.

3. When you are done, click on **Exit preview**; this is the last icon on the menu.

Adding more pages allows you to easily organize the content within a site; by default, sites use **Top navigation**, meaning links will be shown horizontally, but this also limits the amount of links you can use, especially on small screens.

If you are planning on adding more than one or two pages to your site, it might be best to use **Side navigation**. To toggle between navigation styles, follow these steps:

1. Hover over the top header

2. Click on the Navigation settings icon located on the left:

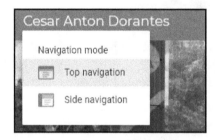

3. Click on the navigation style you prefer:
   - **Top navigation**: This is the default setting with links placed horizontally to the right of the top header
   - **Side Navigation**: This shows a menu icon on the left of the top header:

Click on the hamburger menu icon to display the navigation panel on the left-hand side; links will be placed vertically:

In this section, we learned how to add more pages to our site and also how to toggle between navigation styles. I think your site is now ready to be published. Proceed to the next section to learn how to do this.

Publishing a site

Publishing allows you to decide at which point a site is ready to be seen by its audience. All the changes you make to a site project are stored in real time, but these changes are not made public until the site is published.

This means that you and other collaborators can continue making changes to a site without worrying about the users being able to see a work in progress. Once these changes are ready, just click on **Publish** to update the published version.

To publish a site, follow these steps:

1. Click **Publish** on the top-right menu. You'll see the following **Publish your site** dialog box:

2. Type a temporary address for the site. We will learn how to use a custom one later.

3. Click **MANAGE** to define who can access this site:

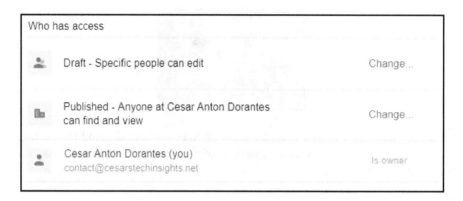

1. Click **Change** next to **Draft** to define who can see the draft, and select one of the available options. By default, only specific people can see the draft:

2. Click **Change** next to **Published** to define who can see the published version of your site. This allows you to choose whether this is a private site for internal use, a private site for clients and partners, or a public site:

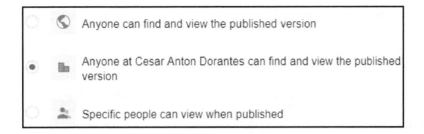

3. Click **Save** to apply your changes.

4. If your site is for private use, enable **Request public search engines to not display my site**.

5. Click **Publish**.

All changes made to the site after publishing will not be visible to the public until the site is published again.

Click on the arrow next to the **Publish** button to show the **Publish options**:

- **Publish settings**: This will allow you to update the web address and enable or disable the request for search engines not to display this site
- **View publisher site**: Use this option to open the published version of the site on a new tab
- **Unpublish**: This option will block users from seeing the site, and only editors will be able to access it until it's published again

In this section, you learned how to define who can access your site and how to publish it; in the next section, you will learn to use custom URLs on Google Sites.

Mapping custom URLs

At this point, you can start using your site, but the default address might seem too long and hard to remember. Giving your site a custom URL makes it easier for users to find it or remember it, and it also makes your site look more professional.

For private sites, you usually don't need to worry too much about having a fancy URL, but public sites look more professional and are easier to remember when they have custom addresses.

G Suite allows you to map custom URLs to your sites' projects to make it easier to write and remember than the default `http://sites.google.com/a/yourdomain.com/yoursitename` pattern. G Suite allows you to map up to 2,000 custom site addresses in your domain.

To map a custom URL to a site, follow these steps from the administrator's home page:

1. Click **Apps**.
2. Click **G Suite**.
3. Click **Sites**.
4. Click **Web Address Mapping**.
5. Click **Add a new web address mapping:**

6. Confirm that the **URL Format** is set to **new Sites**.
7. Type the name of your site in the **Site Location** field. This is the default URL of the site.
8. Type the custom **Web Address** you want for this site—for example: `products.cesarstechinsight.net`.

9. If you have more than one domain on this account, you can select the one you want to use for this page by clicking on the current domain name and selecting the one you want from the drop-down menu.
10. Click **ADD MAPPING** to apply changes.

Now that you know how to set up a basic site and give it a custom URL, proceed to the next section to learn how to integrate Google Sites with G Suite tools.

Integrating Drive documents with Sites

Sites has the ability to seamlessly integrate with any Drive document on a website. You can take advantage of this to create sections of the site that can be easily maintained by members of the team by simply updating the right document.

This ability makes Google Sites a very flexible and powerful tool; you can easily create catalogs or documentation that can be easily maintained by different members of the organization.

Google Sites has the same real-time collaboration capabilities that you see on Google Drive documents, and this means that when multiple collaborators are working on the site at the same time, they can see who is doing what, in real time:

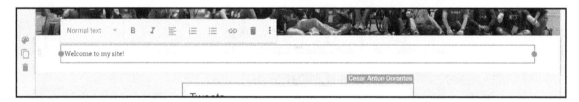

To continue with our example, let's use this feature to create public access to a document that holds your CV. To do that, follow these steps:

1. Create a new page called `My Curriculum`, using the steps we learned about in the *Adding pages* section.
2. Validate that the new **My Curriculum** section is selected so that you can start editing:

3. Click on the **Insert** menu:

4. Click on the **Docs** button.
5. Click on the file (or files) you wish to embed in the site:

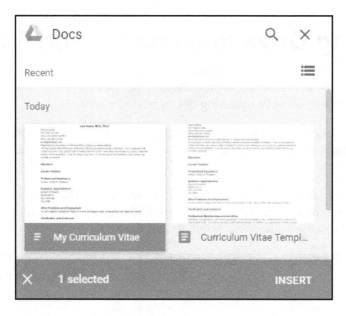

6. Click **INSERT** to add the documents to the page.
7. Adjust the relative size of the documents by dragging the blue dots. You can use this to give each document more relative vertical space so that visitors can read it with more ease:

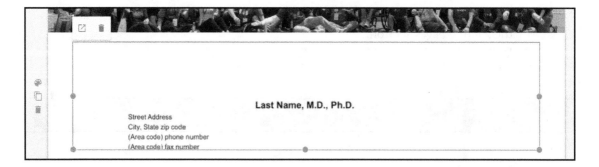

8. Confirm how it looks on different devices using the **Preview** tool:

Document changes are published in real time; this means that any change to a document that's embedded on the site will be visible for the next user that accesses this site.

The editing rights are handled independently between documents and the site itself, so the people working on maintaining the documents don't need to be the same as the ones who are responsible for the site.

You can allow members outside the organization to edit a document without the risk of them using those privileges to make changes on the site.

Summary

Congratulations on finishing this final chapter! You are now capable of creating websites using Google Sites.

You learned how to create new site projects and how to add and style elements to hold text, images, videos, or documents to the site.

Google Sites is simple to use yet powerful and flexible; it empowers users with no coding skills to be able to create their own websites. In this chapter, you learned how to integrate your site with social media platforms such as Twitter by embedding HTML snippets.

You learned how to add more pages to your site so that content can be better organized and accessible for the users; adding pages and sub-pages allows you to create sites as big and as complex as you need to organize your content.

You can now use Google Sites to create a catalog of products and services, as large as you need, and you can also embed payment options with PayPal and integrate with social networks and use it as the sales portal for your organization.

In this chapter, you learned how to preview your site on a small, medium, and large screen before publishing how to control the release of new versions of the website.

We have covered all you need to start creating your own sites, so now I invite you to explore the other features of Google Sites, such as the ability to add maps, slides, forms, and charts.

With all these powerful and flexible tools, you are ready to start creating amazing websites to help your organization grow and prosper.

Other Books You May Enjoy

If you enjoyed this book, you may be interested in these other books by Packt:

Google Cloud Platform Administration
Ranjit Singh Thakurratan

ISBN: 9781788624350

- Understand all GCP Compute components
- Deploy and manage multiple GCP storage options
- Manage and utilize the networking resources offered by GCP
- Explore the functionalities and features of the GCP Container
- Understand the workings of GCP operations such as monitoring and error reporting
- Discover an immune GCP using its identity and security options

Mastering Office 365 Administration
Thomas Carpe, Nikkia Carter, Alara Rogers

ISBN: 9781787288638

- Get an understanding of the vast Office 365 feature set
- Learn how workloads and applications interact and integrate with each other
- Connect PowerShell to various Office 365 services and perform tasks.
- Learn to manage Skype for Business Online
- Get support and monitor Office 365 service health
- Manage and administer identities and groups efficiently

Leave a review - let other readers know what you think

Please share your thoughts on this book with others by leaving a review on the site that you bought it from. If you purchased the book from Amazon, please leave us an honest review on this book's Amazon page. This is vital so that other potential readers can see and use your unbiased opinion to make purchasing decisions, we can understand what our customers think about our products, and our authors can see your feedback on the title that they have worked with Packt to create. It will only take a few minutes of your time, but is valuable to other potential customers, our authors, and Packt. Thank you!

Index